To: Erik

Hope this brings you a little closer to Him.

In His Service,

David Hammond

POEMS FOR THE Heart of God

a Daily Devotional & Spiritual Guide

BY
DARRELL HAUSMANN

Scriptures are taken from the Spirit-Filled Life Bible. Copyright 1991 by Thomas Nelson, Inc. Used by permission. All rights reserved.

Direct quotations from the Bible appear in bold type.

Poems: For the Heart of God
A Daily Devotional and Spiritual Guide
ISBN 0-88144-215-1
Copyright © 2003 by
Rev. Darrell Hausmann
Whitewing Ministries International

Printed in the United States of America. All rights reserved under International Copyright Law. Contents and/or cover may not be reproduced in whole or in part in any form without the express written consent of the author.

Presented to
Erin Kate Ward
oops!! ~~Uncle Skip & Aunt Sue~~

By

Uncle Skip & Aunt Sue

Date

3/6/05

Occasion

I (and Jesus) love you!

Dedication

I would like to take this space to say thank you first, to my Father God, The Head of my house, who brought me out of darkness and into the light of His love. Without Him there would have been no reason to write. Then, to those who have been such an inspiration for me, not only while working on this project, but in ministry and in life, my family.

My mother, Bernice Hausmann-Doughty, now gone Home, for loving me when I wasn't very lovable and for passing down her poem genes:

Pop Doughty for being my father longer than my dad was and for loving me as his own;

My wife Ellen for following me around the world as I have pursued the call of God on my life, for being a constant encouragement and for giving us two wonderful children;

My son Josh, who is too quickly becoming a man, but a son who a father could not be more proud of and one who daily reminds me of the heart of God;

My daughter Lia, the beautiful young lady who contributes more to my life that I could every say. A constant reminder in my ear, "Daddy, write your book."

To Greg, the son who was gone for so long and has returned to my heart, what a jewel you are. Thank all of you for loving me. A man could not be more blessed.

Contents

January..8

Feburary...23

March...38

April..53

May...68

June..84

July...99

August..114

September...130

October..145

November..160

December..175

January 1

Psalm 119:105 "Your word is a lamp to my feet and a light to my path."

Today I will remember Lord to keep you in my heart and mind,
Walking forward Lord and never looking behind;
To enter today with Your Spirit as my guide;
Not looking to yesterday as a place where I can hide;
But looking to You Lord, the One who leads my way;
You Lord, only You to guide me through this day.

January 2

Psalm 37:3 "Trust in the Lord, and do good; Dwell in the land, and feed on His faithfulness."

I know that I can trust You Lord, Your grace is never ending,
Your love for me will never fail, in spite my failures pending;
Valleys low or mountains high, I still will praise Your name;
You are the Lord of then and now not changing, but the same.
Today I give myself to you, to guide my path to good;
To trust, to dwell, to feed, to live the life I should.

January 3

Prov. 27:2 "Let another man praise you, and not your own mouth; A stranger, and not your own lips."

Only You Lord, in all creation deserve the praise of grace,
Let all things that speak of good, be pointed to Your face,
Let my heart be humbled Lord, for another man to say,
He walks, he looks, he lives his life, along the narrow way,
That I might be Your light of life, Your message in my walk,
That I might lift Your name on high in living and in talk.

January 4

Prov. 21:3 "To do righteousness and justice is more acceptable to the Lord than sacrifice."

Help me be a living light of Your compassion, mercy, grace;
That others may see Your justice in the way I take my place.
That living life for You, Oh Lord, is a sacrifice of call,
That righteousness and justice reign, a living call to all,
Remember Lord, accepting me, glean away my pride,
I stand in awe, that You would chose to stand here by my side.

January 5

1 Cor. 3:16 "Do you not know that you are the temple of God and that the Spirit of God dwells in you?"

I am the house that is blessed with the presence of all that is You,
Help me incorporate today, in this temple, all that is worthy and true.
You have made me acceptable in Your eyes Oh Lord, a worthy place to dwell,
Help me be a house of hope for others today, a house where all is well,
Let this house be an example to those who seek Your peace,
A lighthouse of Your love and a grace that does not cease.

January 6

1 Cor. 13:1 "Though I speak with the tongues of men and of angels, but have not love, I have become sounding brass or a clanging cymbal."

There is no love like yours Father, but help me understand I am created like You,
That if I allow it to be so, today, Your love through me, may touch not just a few,
That I might be the light of Your love in a world that emits a hardened tone,
To turn the hurting toward You, that Your grace may be easily shown.
Grant me today, O Lord, a tongue that emits a sound pleasing to You,
A tongue that brings forth peace to a troubled soul, a heart to renew.

January 7

2 Cor. 5:1 "For we know that if our earthly house, this tent, is destroyed, we have a building from God, a house not made with hands, eternal in the heavens."

Thank You Lord for the peace You give in my heart through the assurance of You,
That I may not be concerned with this building or things in my passing through,
But that I might cling to the wonder of your grace and the promises of a better land,
One that You have prepared for me and all who are guided by the Carpenter's hand.
Help me to glory in You as I walk through the hours of this day,
Knowing that in Your time I'll live eternal in a place with no decay.

January 8

2 Cor. 5:17 "Therefore, if anyone is in Christ, he is a new creation; old things have passed away; behold, all things have become new."

How wonderful it is to know that You have forgotten what laid before,
To put the past away in Your remembrance, to open Heaven's door,
To love me just the way I am, created to Your call,
Not holding me accountable for the darkness of my fall.
From dust to life, lost to found, Your grace has made me new,
I'll walk today, one day in time and keep my eyes on You.

January 9

2 Cor. 12:9 "And He said to me, 'My grace is sufficient for you, for My strength is made perfect in weakness.'"

If today I begin to feel down, unloved, downtrodden, lowly or lost,
Help me remember Lord, who I am in You and Your sacrificial cost;
You have provided for me Lord, all that I need today,
To enter into Your hands, to be molded, a diamond from clay;
Help me understand Lord, my character made by grace,
That my weakness perfects my strength as I gaze upon Your face.

January 10

Gal. 3:28 "There is neither Jew nor Greek, there is neither slave nor free, there is neither male nor female; for you are all one in Christ Jesus."

As I walk through this day O Lord, help my heart smile at all who surround me,
Let all see Your love in me that I, from all prejudice, may turn and flee;
That each may see the value You have placed on all created kind,
Love for all and all for love and peace each one will find;
That as this day will end for me and darkness starts the night,
That all may have seen the goodness in You and they, precious in Your sight.

January 11

Eph. 1:7 "In Him we have redemption through His blood, the forgiveness of sins, according to the riches of His grace."

Thank You Lord for being my redeemer and standing in the gap for my eternal race,
For Your sacrifice of the Cross, Your resurrection power, the gift of grace;
I am rich in the glory of You, let it shine from me as I walk in Your steps today,
Help me be the light of Your forgiveness and love in everything I say;
That the honor of You will be lifted up and the glory of Your kingdom shine,
I will honor You with my life today, I will be today for You, a sign.

January 12

James 4:10 "Humble yourselves in the sight of the Lord, and He will lift you up."

What is it to say that I am anything of myself alone,
That the pride of my heart may be uncovered and shown;
That only You may lift up the good of my day,
May the words of Your Spirit imprint my heart to stay;
And leave me and those around a greater sense of sight,
For we are blinded, but in You we are lifted up and set aright.

January 13

John 16:33 "These things I have spoken to you, that in Me you may have peace. In the world you will have tribulation; but be of good cheer, I have overcome the world."

What a comforting thought to know that I will not face today alone,
But that with every challenge that comes, victory in You is shown;
I will walk through every valley knowing Your peace goes before me,
And I will sing praises as each mountain falls away to the "sea."
For there is no other God like You Who created us to overcome,
In it all, let it be seen who You are to all, and not just some.

January 14

1 Peter 2:18 "Servants, be submissive to your masters with all fear, not only to the good and gentle, but also to the harsh."

A new day brings about a fresh outlook to those I must see,
Help me start with the kindness and grace You called me to be;
To give the best of my hand and a heart called of You,
Remembering that each day You give starts new;
And each time I put forth my heart and mind to test,
That I realize my part is in You and Your part the rest.

January 15

John 15:7 "If you abide in Me and My words abide in you, you will ask what you desire, and it shall be done for you."

Today I will abide in You Lord and follow Your word as my guide,
I will walk in Your way, stand boldly for You as we walk side by side,
I will ask only that You fill me with Your presence as I live out today,
There is no promise that You cannot keep as I kneel before You and pray.
I will say that You are my all in all and proclaim Your goodness to the lost,
You have promised me those things that are mine and have already paid the cost.

January 16

Phil. 4:13 "I can do all things through Christ who strengthens me."

When the day comes, trials begin and there seems no end in site,
Help me remember that it is by Your Spirit not power or might:
That brings me into the presence of what can and can not be done,
For the power is not of myself, but the power is in the Son,
Who came to give me grace in this and all days,
And victory through His Spirit, who in my heart stays.

January 17

Phil. 4:19 "And my God shall supply all your need according to His riches in glory by Christ Jesus."

What need do I have that I cannot depend on You for supply?
That my mind would even ponder that on You I cannot rely.
All that was created is from You, that I might live without fear,
Knowing that regardless of lack's perception, You are near.
And that all that I am and all that I have comes from Your grace,
That I might live in abundance eternally and even in this place.

January 18

Prov. 3:5 "Trust in the Lord with all your heart, And lean not on your own understanding."

Help me today Lord, to trust in You in whatever may come my way,
Give me the confidence to listen to Your Spirit's direction and obey.
If I am willing and obedient I will be blessed with the good of the land,
And when the goodness comes, those around will see You in my stand;
That Your name may be glorified, lifted up and praised,
And the hearts of men will be molded, encouraged, and raised.

January 19

Luke 6:31 "And just as you want men to do to you, you also do to them likewise."

Today is another day You have given me to fill with love and grace,
To look toward another with a smile on my face;
To bring the joy of knowing who I am in You,
And to remember to my own heart, be true,
That I might reap the blessings of You and man,
Being the light of Your love to all that I can.

January 20

John 12:46 "I have come as a light into the world, that whoever believes in Me should not abide in darkness."

You are the Bright and Morning Star that lights up the darkness around me,
The One who lights the path of my day, that I might not stumble, but see;
I do believe, so I give this day to You and abide in Your light,
That though mountains may stand to turn the day to night,
I will not falter in my step nor stumble by the weight of fear,
Because You are the tower over the mountain and You are here.

January 21

Romans 12:10 "Be kindly affectionate to one another with brotherly love, in honor giving preference to one another."

One more day to be warmed by You in a world that is cold,
A day that Your love will help my countenance stand bold;
To be the light of Your kindness and the honor of Your command.
To love the un-lovable I may face, but hold to my stand;
That I may be the light and affection of Your love today,
And show a path of honor in walking in Your way.

January 22

Genesis 1:26 "Then God said, 'Let Us make man in Our image, according to Our likeness; let them have dominion over the fish of the sea, over the birds of the air, and over the cattle, over all the earth and over every creeping thing that creeps on the earth."

Lord, help me today to understand the responsibility I have in dominion,
That I might not dwell in my own thoughts or my own opinion;
But that I would create the image of You in my daily walk,
And that You would be blessed by the benevolence of my talk;
Remind me that Your creation in me is the image of Your heart,
That goodness and mercy in me may show Your divine impart.

January 23

Genesis 1:1 "In the beginning God created the heavens and the earth."

Lord how majestic and loving You are to make me part of Your plan,
Of all the glory defined in Your creation of me and all human clan;
Help me remember today, the power of divine interface,
That I might be reminded of Your never ending grace;
You created all that stands before You to praise Your name,
Creating me in the image of You, that I might stand the same.

January 24

Genesis 8:22 "While the earth remains, Seedtime and harvest, Cold and heat, Winter and summer, And day and night Shall not cease."

While the earth remains I will sow seeds of Your promise and Your grace,
That I might become fruitful in harvest while in this earthly place,
To sow the seed of Your promise in the soil of my need,
Yet refrain from bowing to the world's quest and greed.
That ever act of my being is a delight in the life that I live,
For no other act is worthy of the promise that You give.

January 25

Psalm 16:11 "You will show me the path of life; In Your presence is fullness of joy; At Your right hand are pleasures forevermore."

Thank You Father, that You show me the path I should walk,
That You not only show me, but You walk along and we talk;
Your presence at my side brings me a day full of joy,
Like a young child that is enthralled with his favorite toy.
My day will be like a beautiful flower warmed by rays of light,
Praising You with the beauty of Your creation and might.

January 26

Psalm 19:14 "Let the words of my mouth and the meditation of my heart Be acceptable in Your sight, O Lord, my strength and my Redeemer."

Let my words today, Lord, be words that will glorify You only,
Words that may bring hope to those lost and lonely;
Words that would bring peace to a barren desert land,
For change to come, bettered by Your hand.
You are my strength and the redeemer who sees me through,
May the meditation of my heart, remind others of You.

January 27

Psalm 37:3 "Trust in the Lord, and do good; Dwell in the land, and feed on His faithfulness. Delight yourself also in the Lord, And He shall give you the desires of your heart."

I will trust You today with all that I am and all that You want me to be,
And I will dwell in Your presence as You walk with me and lead me;
The desire of my heart is to know Your will in my life at every turn,
To be filled with Your Spirit that my heart will be open to learn;
All that is good that comes from You, moldable by Your hand,
That You may be seen in me, as in Your grace I stand.

January 28

Psalm 46:1 "God is our refuge and strength, A very present help in trouble."

Your care for me encourages me as I walk through the day,
Knowing that I can depend on You and what You say.
You are the Refuge I seek when daily challenges fare,
Believing that I am secure in You, not tossed hither and there,
Nor left alone to face mountains, knowing You're the One,
Who constantly stands by my side till each day is done.

January 29

Psalm 51:10 "Create in me a clean heart, O God, And renew a steadfast spirit within me."

Today Lord, I ask You again to help me keep my thoughts pure and true,
To be that image, to be that light that exhibits the character of You,
To stand steadfast in a world that is moving toward spiritual fall,
Keep my heart clean, pure, and fixed on You through it all.
That I may be a winsome example for the one in spiritual loss,
And be a guide of grace to their understanding of the Cross.

January 30

Psalm 84:11 "For the Lord God is a sun and shield; The Lord will give grace and glory; No good thing will He withhold From those who walk uprightly."

I wake up each morning knowing that You are the Protector of my life,
And that whatever comes my way, because of You, I am free from strife;
Because You are the Creator, the One who shields my day,
The One who stands in the gap when trials come my way;
The good of the day I can see as mine because I walk the narrow path,
But for those who come against me, their reward is Your wrath.

January 31

Psalm 89:15 "Blessed are the people who know the joyful sound! They walk, O Lord, in the light of Your countenance."

Today I will be blessed because I lift up my voice to You in praise,
Your light will shine upon me because it is Your banner that I raise;
I will be among the people who walk in the light of Your grace,
Among those who call You Lord and magnify You in this place.
There is no more joyful noise than the sound of Your name,
And to hear Your voice in return, today, forever, the same.

February 1

Psalm 91:2 "I will say of the Lord, 'He is my refuge and my fortress; My God, in Him I will trust.'"

Each day that I trust in You, I stand at the mountain top of grace,
And each day I call You to stand by me in my race;
That I may reach the crown that You have promised me at the end;
That You and You alone are the One in whom I can depend.
I will trust You today to lead me, guide me , protect me from a fall,
That I may stand strong for You and speak worth of Your call.

February 2

Psalm 108:13 "Through God we will do valiantly; For it is He who shall tread down our enemies."

What a mighty God You are that You would stand for me in their way,
That You would tread them down, moving each mountain far away;
A valiant God of peace, yet taking my place in each day's fight,
Standing as a fortress in me as You put our enemies to flight.
Through You Lord , this day will be won, no matter the test,
And through You Lord , no matter the test, I will rest.

February 3

Psalm 145:2 "Every day I will bless You, And I will praise Your name forever and ever."

You, O Lord have given me another day to sing of Your power and might,
Remembering that each day brings Your creation greatness to my sight;
That I may continually lift up my heart to You in confession,
That You are Lord and King and the glory of my salvation.
Your name will forever be enthroned on my heart and mind,
I will bless You with praise and walk as not blind.

February 4

Prov. 9:10 "The fear of the Lord is the beginning of wisdom, And the knowledge of the Holy One is understanding."

You promise wisdom for those who ask Lord, so I ask,
Knowing that gaining knowledge is only part of the task.
I will listen to what You will say and will take Your lead,
Knowing that the wisdom of Your Spirit is all I need.
To walk through the day, not walking a lie,
But in truth I will walk, praising my Savior on high.

February 5

Prov, 12:15 "The way of a fool is right in his own eyes, But he who heeds counsel is wise."

Help me walk wisely today Lord, not in my own way, but in Your will,
That I might draw to me Your character and my heart still.
I wish not to be regarded as a fool, but righteous in Your eyes,
That I may be counted as those in You who walk as wise.
For You are to me today as always before,
The One who lifts me up and needed more and more.

February 6

Prov. 12:26 "The righteous should choose his friends carefully, For the way of the wicked leads them astray."

I have been made righteous by the life in Your Son,
Acceptable in Your eyes through the blood of the Holy One.
So help me Father, to honor the call of Your voice,
By guiding me wisely to the friends of Your choice.
Yet help me be open to love all that You call in life,
That I may be an example to avert their fall, their strife.

February 7

Prov. 15:4 "A wholesome tongue is a tree of life, But perverseness in it breaks the spirit."

Help my tongue today be life to those who hear,
And that the sound of my voice be pleasing in Your ear;
That the words of my mouth may be a light to those lost,
To enlighten their heart and mind to the eternal cost.
May each heart be lifted by the words that I say,
That I may honor and glorify You in every way.

February 8

Prov. 16:9 "A man's heart plans his way, But the Lord directs his steps."

Lord , open my heart to see the path You have set before me,
Knowing that each step I take is a choice that is free.
In the freedom of You there is choice in the direction that I take,
So I pray my steps are for You and You alone the choice I make.
And in the freedom of my heart, I seek for You to dwell,
So that in each step I take in You the world may tell—That I am Yours.

February 9

Prov: 27:19 "As in water face reflects face, So a man's heart reveals the man."

You are my Father, Your are my grace, help me reflect this in You today,
And may my heart show in deed, the same as my lips would say.
When I look in the water, may it reflect the likeness of You;
So my heart may reveal a man that is true.
May the image that is set before me, be an image of grace,
That I might see in me, victory in You ,in this place.

February 10

Haggai 1:7 "Thus says the Lord of hosts: 'Consider your ways!'"

What should I consider today other than my walk with You;
What matters more than Your guidance that carries me through?
That I should consider anything else to give;
Other than Your way, in my heart, where You live?
I will confirm the path where I follow Your lead,
And not stray from Your goodness in word or deed.

February 11

Prov. 28:6 "Better is the poor who walks in his integrity, Than one perverse in his ways, though he be rich."

There are those all around me who claim a better life,
But they flounder in their way through sickness and strife.
What they have is for but a time, then gone away,
But I have You Lord to sustain me throughout each day.
I gather not those things around me that call me to pride,
But those things that are forever and draw me to Your side.

February 12

Prov. 30:5 "Every word of God is pure; He is a shield to those who put their trust in Him."

I am so blessed that I can depend on Your promises,
That every word from You is truth that admonishes;
And lifts me up to a higher place of protection,
Knowing that Your promise is a shield of perfection;
Nothing can take away the power of Your purity,
And in it all, a promise of peace and surety.

February 13

Eccl. 12:13 "Let us hear the conclusion of the whole matter: Fear God and keep His commandments, For this is man's all."

There is no other reason for this day, than to keep Your law,
Though I have been redeemed by the Son, redeemed from the fall.
I am not free to call things by volition of my own,
In time what matters is that I stand before Your throne;
Knowing that I keep my eyes daily, on Your face;
And that in the end I will dwell in Your promised place.

February 14

1 John 4:18 "There is no fear in love; but perfect love casts out fear, because fear involves torment, But he who fears has not been made perfect in love."

Today my heart is bound to love, because of what He's done,
Not called to hurt, but cast off fear and keep our hearts as one.
Today is called a special day to celebrate His name,
A call to all to walk in love, to remember why He came.
There is no greater love than His, the Master at the gate,
That's why He came, so great a love, to now secure our fate.

February 15

Isaiah 60:1 "Arise, shine; For your light has come! And the glory of the Lord is risen upon you."

You are wondrous Lord, that You could care that I wake to such a day,
That the light of You would bring a presence beyond what I can say;
That Your glory would spend a moment to shine upon me,
That Your glory would care in what state I may be;
So I do arise in the name of Your Son of Light,
That the glory of Him may fill me today with His power and might.

February 16

Jer. 17: 7 "Blessed is the man who trusts in the Lord, And whose hope is the Lord."

I look for Your blessings as the day goes on and I see Your good,
That I may walk in Your light and receive those things I could;
Because You bless those that walk in trust,
Not those who walk in worldly lust.
You are the Hope of my day and the One to Whom I call,
That no matter what comes, I'll not be subject to a fall.

February 17

1 Tim. 1:5 "Now the purpose of the commandment is love from a pure heart, from a good conscience, and from sincere faith."

Father I pray for a pure heart that will be a light for You today,
That as I walk through it, every word I speak will glorify Your way.
That no purpose other than that of good conscience will prevail,
And all that I do will the name of Jesus hail.
For to walk in any other way may cause a heart to woe,
But to draw close to You may to another, Jesus show.

February 18

2 Tim. 1:7 "For God has not given us a spirit of fear, but of power and of love and of a sound mind."

Because of Your love one more day will be lived without fear,
Knowing that You are one in me; You are near.
While others may struggle through the trials of the day,
I will stand on the promises of Your word, what You say;
I will live today with a clear heart with actions kind,
And receive the power and peace of a sound mind.

February 19

Jer. 23:23 "'Am I a God near at hand', says the Lord, 'And not a God afar off?'"

Let my life answer that You are a God that always stands near,
That no matter what things may seem, Your presence is clear.
Some would say that You are far away,
But they do not know You Lord in a personal way.
I will live forever with peace in my hand,
Knowing that You are with me in places I stand.

February 20

Jer. 29:11 "For I know the thoughts that I think toward you, says the Lord, thoughts of peace and not of evil, to give you a future and a hope."

You in my thoughts today gives me the peace I long to feel,
Knowing that I am in Your thoughts is a bonding seal;
That keeps me on task in the middle road of life,
And draws me to strength to face evil or strife,
Because I know that Your promise is true,
And that the future of peace and hope is in You.

February 21

Jer: 31:3 "The Lord has appeared of old to me saying: 'Yes, I have loved you with an everlasting love; Therefore with loving kindness I have drawn you."

There is no love nor kindness like Yours that I see,
That can draw any conclusion, but Your love for me.
Today is no different that yesterday or tomorrow,
For You will redeem me from any hurt or sorrow.
For which I will praise forever Your name,
Yesterday, today, and tomorrow the same.

February 22

Jer. 33:3 "Call to Me, and I will answer you, and show you great and mighty things, which you do not know."

I will call You throughout the day for Your wisdom's guide,
You will call back to lead me and nothing to hide,
That I may be lifted up to You and my path shown,
Knowing that You walk ahead and I am not alone.
To enter and leave the day as set out for me,
To glorify Your name for all others to see.

February 23

Lam. 3:25 "The Lord is good to those who wait for Him, To the soul who seeks Him."

I will wait for You and in that time I will seek You,
So You will be with me, the day guide me through;
I will receive Your goodness each day I live,
For to You all glory and thanksgiving I give.
In seeking You I will not be pulled from Your chosen way,
But will wait upon You Lord for Your blessings today.

February 24

Isaiah 40:31 "But those who wait on the Lord Shall renew their strength; They shall mount up with wings like eagles, They shall run and not be weary, They shall walk and not faint."

Though I may be weary I count You as my wings,
The Lord my Savior, my King of kings;
To lift me up from the pit of earth's scorn,
To stand me tall and straight in Your image I am born.
I will fly through the day on Your eagles wings,
I know that I have victory, whatever this day brings.

February 25

Isaiah 43:2 "When you pass through the waters, I will be with you; And through the rivers, they shall not overflow you. When you walk through the fire, you shall not be burned, Nor shall the flame scorch you."

Could anything be more promising than the promise of You,
That whatever trials come I'll make it through?
For there is no other power that in eternity's time,
Could cover or shield, no God but mine.
I can face the day in the confidence of your power,
Knowing that I am covered at any given hour.

February 26

Isaiah 53:6 "All we like sheep have gone astray; We have turned, every one, to his own way; And the Lord has laid on Him the iniquity of us all."

While we have strayed, we have been set straight by the blood of the Lamb,
And I praise You for making me in Your image and what I am.
That You would love me and make this sacrifice for me,
Is beyond what I could ever comprehend or see,
But I lay my life before You and pray to be a light,
That I may lift up others who are precious in Your sight.

February 27

Ezekiel 36:27 "I will put My Spirit within you and cause you to walk in My statutes, and you will keep My judgements and do them."

What a wonderful God of mercy and grace You are to me,
That You would care to teach me how I should be;
That You would dwell with me in this temple made by You,
And guide my ways to Your statutes be true.
Not only will I keep them, but I will be a guide,
That others may see the path that leads to Your side.

February 28

Joshua 1:9 "Have I not commanded you? Be strong and of good courage; do not be afraid, nor be dismayed, for the Lord your God is with you wherever you go."

Today is another day that You have given me to trust in You,
I will be strong, have courage, because You will see me through.
I have this treasure inside that fills my day with praise,
The treasure of You , the joy of You where my heart stays.
I will not be afraid no matter what challenge may fall,
For in my heart and on my lips , Your name will be my call.

February 29
(Leap Year)

Zephaniah 2:3 "Seek the Lord, all you meek of the earth, Who have upheld His justice, seek righteousness, seek humility. It may be that you will be hidden In the day of the Lord's anger."

Everyday, Lord, bring me into the company of the meek,
Bath me in humility for pride is for the weak;
I will seek Your righteousness and be Your light;
I will honor Your statutes and walk the right;
And I will fall in the threshold of Your grace;
As I stand in the shadow of my eternal place.

March 1

1 Samuel 17:47 "Then all this assembly shall know that the Lord does not save with sword and spear; for the battle is the Lord's, and He will give you into our hands."

Whatever trial I may face today, my faith will move the mountain,
For You O Lord are life to me, my watering fountain,
That never runs dry and always brings about the victory,
For You are the God who has delivered throughout history.
I will stand before those assembled around me today,
And be an example of David, standing firm living Your way.

March 2

1 Kings 9:3 "And the Lord said to him: I have heard your prayer and your supplication that you have made before Me; I have consecrated this house which you have built to put My name there forever, and My eyes and My heart will be there perpetually.'"

I am happy to start this day knowing that Your eyes are on me,
And that Your heart is set upon me perpetually,
Never leaving this house that I am constantly repairing,
And knowing that Your grace is one of sparing;
Your name is written upon my heart and mind,
And through the day with You it's constant peace I'll find.

March 3

1 Kings 18:21 "And Elijah came to all people, and said, 'How long will you falter between two opinions? If the Lord is God, follow Him; if Baal, follow him. But the people answered him not a word."

Lord, help me let not this day be a day of falter,
But a day that I would be turned toward Your alter;
With praise as to who You are in my vision,
A day filled with the presence of Godly decision,
That I would follow You in all that I do,
And show those around me the God that is true.

March 4

1 Chron. 4:10 "And Jabez called on the God of Israel saying, 'Oh, that You may bless me indeed, and enlarge my territory, that Your hand would be with me, and that You would keep me from evil, that I may not cause pain!' So God granted him what he requested."

Lord, hear my prayer today and enlarge my territory,
Not of things, but opportunity to tell the Good News story.
That in keeping You before my day Your grace may fall;
To show the lives of many, Your love for them all.
And grant me a tongue that would cause no heart to stumble,
Giving me the strength to walk in love, to be humble.

March 5

1 Chron. 29:11 "Yours, O Lord, is the greatness, The power and the glory, The victory and the majesty; For all that is in heaven and in earth is Yours; Yours is the kingdom, O Lord, And You are exalted as head over all."

How You are exalted in my eyes and above all things,
And how much You touch my heart and it sings;
Knowing that all that exists, exists from Your creation,
And that I am blessed to share the daily celebration,
Of being part of the family of You the Most High,
And knowing that on all that is You , I can rely.

March 6

Job 4:6 "Is not your reverence your confidence? And the integrity of your ways your hope?"

You are my Father and the confidence that guides my way,
And the Spirit inside that silently guides these lips that say;
You are the truth that binds my speech that shows Your light,
No matter what the world may bring, no matter the plight;
For there is no other hope than the hope that we live,
In You and in Your way and in the integrity we hold to give.

March 7

Psalm 101:3 "I will set nothing wicked before my eyes; I hate the work of those who fall away; It shall not cling to me."

Lift my eyes up to You O Lord, that Your Spirit not be grieved,
And keep the focus of my day on You lest I be deceived.
Let not those things grievous to Your Spirit, enter my heart,
Continue to strengthen me that I may be consistent in my part.
To keep the joy of my day focused on Your face,
And all that calls of You be tempered by Your grace.

March 8

2 Chron. 5:13 "Indeed it came to pass, when the trumpeters and singers were as one, to make one sound to be heard in praising and thanking the Lord, and when they lifted up their voice with the trumpets and cymbals and instruments of music, and praised the Lord, saying: 'For He is good, For His mercy endures forever,' that the house, the house of the Lord, was filled with a cloud,"

Today is the day to praise you and lift up Your name,
Give us strength and wisdom to praise in unity, all the same;
That the music of our hearts will be instruments of praise,
Lifted up to the Most High our voices raise;
To sing with joy that our thanksgiving may be loud,
Reaching to heaven–experiencing the cloud.

March 9

2 Chron. 7:14 "If My people who are called by My name will humble themselves, and pray and seek My face, and turn from their wicked ways, then I will hear from heaven, and will forgive their sin and heal their land."

I will seek Your face today and turn toward You,
And humble myself to do what You have called me to do;
I will pray and know You will hear my prayer,
Because You are a God that is merciful and fair.
Look around and see those who seek Your hand,
Forgive us all that fall short and heal our land.

March 10

Job 5:8 "But as for me, I would seek God, And to God I would commit my cause"

Truly You are worthy to praise, honor, worship and commit my day,
For You alone are the creation of all, there is no other way;
And I will seek Your face as the light of my hope,
Knowing full well that You are the reason I cope,
With a world that challenges the existence of my being,
But believing Your Spirit is the eye of my seeing.

March 11

Job 28:28 "And to man He said, 'Behold, the fear of the Lord, that is wisdom, And to depart from evil is understanding.'"

The sun came up this morning and I saw You in it,
And a cloud was formed as a throne upon which You sit;
To look upon our hearts and to see our way,
Would we follow You or would we have our own say;
Will the fear of You Lord bring wisdom to bare?
Will we depart from evil and grant You our fare?

March 12

Psalm 2:7 "I will declare the decree; The Lord has said to Me, You are My Son, Today I have begotten You."

The day is brightened by the light of Your Son,
May I praise You forever and all that He's done.
May I understand that I am begotten too,
This day is given for Your purpose by You;
That I too might declare a decree,
That I am in You and You are in me.

March 13

Psalm 5:12 "For You, O Lord, will bless the righteous; With favor You will surround him as with a shield."

I am blessed because I am righteous because of Your Son,
And I will lift up His name, my Savior the only One;
Who can shield me from the trial of the day,
And any other evil that may come my way,
For I can depend on You and stand on Your word,
Because by Your blood I'm in the family—preferred.

March 14

Psalm 9:1 "I will praise You, O Lord, with my whole heart; I will tell of all Your marvelous works."

Today is a new day to glorify Your grace,
In each life that You have called, to run the race;
To tell of Your love in the way I live my life,
To see Your character in the midst of strife;
That all may see the Lord of You in me,
I will be a light, Your light, for all to see.

March 15

Psalm 15;1,2 "Lord, who may abide in Your tabernacle? Who may dwell in Your holy hill? He who walks uprightly, And works righteousness, and speaks the truth in his heart."

I am Your tabernacle Lord, and I will abide in Your holy hill,
Because I will honor You and strive to do Your will.
I will walk uprightly and speak truth from my heart,
And will dwell in You wholly not just in part.
I will be the hands of Your grace today,
And be Your lead so others may find their way.

March 16

Psalm 16:11 "You will show me the path of life; In Your presence is fullness of joy; At Your right hand are pleasures forevermore."

How wonderful You are that You would guide my way,
Into the fullness of joy You have for me today;
That You have created pleasures in which I may live,
And glorify Your joy to others my life may give.
Help me Lord today to be what You would have me to be,
Your light unto others that they might be set free.

March 17

Psalm 25:4,5 "Show me Your ways, O Lord; Teach me Your paths. Lead me in Your truth and teach me, For You are the God of my salvation; On You I wait all the day."

I will listen to Your voice as You show me Your way,
And I will open my heart to Your teaching today;
That I might hear and know the truth of Your word,
And not fail to yield to what I have heard;
For You will lead me today into what is right,
That I might be pleasing in Your way and in Your sight.

March 18

Psalm 26:1,2 "Vindicate me, O Lord, For I have walked in my integrity. I shall not slip. Examine me, O Lord, and prove me; Try my mind and my heart."

I will walk today in what You have placed in me,
I'll not falter in the strength of my integrity;
Prove me Lord, try my heart and mind,
I pray only goodness, mercy, and grace You will find;
That the truth of You is what shines as a light,
And that You will find me worthy in Your sight.

March 19

Psalm 27:1 "The Lord is my light and my salvation; Whom shall I fear? The Lord is the strength of my life; Of whom shall I be afraid?"

The sun has risen and lit up the eastern sky,
It reminds of my Savior who chose to die;
Then rise from the darkness to light up my way,
To take away any fear I may face today.
How wonderful You are to keep me in Your care,
That I may not fear--I will overcome—You will bare.

March 20

Psalm 30:5 "For His anger is but for a moment, His favor is for life; Weeping may endure for a night, But joy comes in the morning."

You are the discipline of my day and Your anger justified,
Thank You for redemption by Your Son, crucified;
Who bore me up to give me favor in Your eyes,
The One whom You sent, the One who justifies.
I will not fear knowing the day I will endure,
And knowing You are my strength, strong and sure.

March 21

Psalm 37:23 "The steps of a good man are ordered by the Lord, And He delights in his way."

The path of my steps are the long and narrow road,
The road that has been set before me and seeds sowed;
That the order of my life is planted in Your way,
And the delight of You is in me today.
I feel the joy of knowing who I am in You,
And in keeping the faith and knowing what is true.

March 22

Psalm 37:40 "And the Lord shall help them and deliver them; He shall deliver them from the wicked, And save them, Because they trust in Him."

I will trust in You because I am part of them,
And I am delivered today because if Him;
Who sits on the throne at Your right hand,
And leads and guides the righteous in the land,
That was given to Satan in the fall,
But has been redeemed through His obedient call.

March 23

Psalm 40:2 "He also brought me up out of a horrible pit, Out of the miry clay, And set my feet upon a rock, And established my steps."

As I face today, I know that You are the rock of my being.
And as I walk forward, I trust that You are my seeing;
That I will find the path of Your honor in today's walk,
To show the love of You in deed and talk;
And show that Your are with me, You are mine;
To trust in, to obey, to be a righteous sign.

March 24

Psalm 48:1 "Great is the Lord, and greatly to be praised In the city of our God, In His holy mountain."

Lord, You are great and greatly to be praised,
For my salvation, Your Son, my Lord, was raised,
That through my faith in Him who set me free;
My life may change as He dwells in me;
And that I may dwell on top of the mountain,
And forever praise Him, my watering fountain.

March 25

Psalm 54:6 "I will freely sacrifice to You; I will praise Your name, O Lord, for it is good."

I will lift up my praise to You because You are always good,
And the sacrifice of praise is nothing less than I should;
Give to the One who has set me upon a rock of singing,
And to who is worthy of the honor I am bringing.
I am blessed as my life is bathed in Your eternal grace,
And as I look to the goodness in my Father's face.

March 26

Matt: 5:14 "You are the light of the world. A city that is set on a hill cannot be hidden."

You have made me, created me to be a light,
Not hidden , but one who is pleasing in Your sight;
To shine with the grace that only comes from You,
That I might be an example of Your chosen few,
From out of the darkness to the light on the hill,
Formed in Your image and called to Your will.

March 27

Matt. 5:43,44 "You have heard that it was said, 'You shall love your neighbor and hate your enemy,' But I say to you, love your enemy, bless those who curse you, do good to those who hate you, and pray for those who spitefully use you and persecute you."

Father, I know that today I'll be called before a throne,
And tested by some, am I truly Your own;
But I know I've been created to stand by Your grace,
And no matter what comes You're the crown of my race.
To set an example of the love of Your Cross,
To be the goodness of You, no matter the loss.

March 28

Matt: 6:7 "And when you pray, do not use vain repetitions as the heathen do. For they think that they will be heard for their many words."

Remind me, as I start my day with You on my mind,
That Your ears are open and Your eyes not blind;
You know and see before I even speak,
The things on my heart, things that I seek.
So help my words be simple in what I might pray,
And always from my heart the things I might say.

March 29

Deut. 6:5 "You shall love the Lord your God with all your heart, with all your soul, and with all your strength."

Today is a new day that You have given me,
To show the love that has set me free;
To walk the life which I confess;
To live out Your grace that I possess,
To show others the hope I have in You;
That from beginning to end, You will see me through.

March 30

Deut. 28:1 "Now it shall come to pass, if you diligently obey the voice of the Lord your God, to observe carefully all His commandments which I commanded you today, that the Lord your God will set you high above all nations of the earth."

I will listen to the sound of Your voice,
And I will honor You as I make each choice,
In the path I walk in my life today;
I will choose to accept, I will choose to obey;
That I may receive the blessings of Your grace;
And be set apart for You as I run my race.

March 31

Numbers 6:24-26 "The Lord bless you and keep you; The Lord make His face shine on you, and be gracious to you; The Lord lift up His countenance upon you, And give you peace."

How wonderful it is to know I am in Your care,
And that I serve a God Whose judgement is fair;
That through the day I will be kept by You,
That all that You say is faithful and true;
That You constantly lift me out of the miry clay,
And that You listen as I lift my heart and pray.

April 1

Judges 6:12 "And the Angel of the Lord appeared to him, and said to him, 'The Lord is with you, you mighty man of valor.'"

What gives me strength to be a man that's bold?
To stand firm in You without seeming cold?
Only the presence of You in my heart can be;
The steadfast love that others may see,
For You are with me and You are strong,
And in You my valor is Your song.

April 2

Ruth 2:12 "The Lord repay your work, and a full reward be given you by the Lord God of Israel, under whose wings you have come for refuge."

The work that I do today, I do for You,
Not of duty, but because my heart is true;
And because of the blessing of Your grace,
And the abundance of Your provision in this place;
I know that I am in the shadow of Your wings;
And have the blessings that Your refuge brings.

April 3

1 Sam. 2:7,8 "The Lord makes poor and makes rich; He brings low and lifts up. He raises the poor from the dust And lifts the beggar from the ash heap, To set them among princes And make them inherit the throne of glory."

I bow before You today, O Lord, mighty in deed,
For You are the God who will meet every need;
You have lifted me up from darkness and dust,
And blessed me with Your love and trust.
You will make me rich as I walk in Your way,
And set me upon Your glory throne, today.

April 4

1 Sam. 12:14 "If you fear the Lord and serve Him and obey His voice, and do not rebel against the commandment of the Lord, then both you and the king who reigns over you will continue following the Lord Your God."

I will honor You today in all that I do and say,
And strive to be an example of Your way;
That I may be a light for those in command,
To assure Your blessings on this land;
That this nation may honor You in the eyes of all,
To be Your voice, to further Your call.

April 5

2 Sam. 7:29 "Now therefore, let it please You to bless the house of Your servant, that it may continue before You forever; for You, O Lord God, have spoken it, and with Your blessing let the house of Your servant be blessed forever."

Father, thank You for blessing my land,
I give thanks for all that comes from Your hand;
I lift my voice to You in honor and praise,
My life, Your temple, to build, to raise.
Your blessing promised as I live for You,
A promised grace to see me through.

April 6

Psalm 119:111 "Your testimonies I have taken as a heritage forever, For they are the rejoicing of my heart."

The words that You speak to my heart are my guide,
The testimony of my spirit walking by Your side;
You are my Father and I am Your created one,
The one You love, saved by Your Son.
I will testify of Your love and grace for me,
And rejoice in You for all the world to see.

April 7

Psalm 119:130 "The entrance of Your words, gives light; It gives understanding to the simple."

I will enter the day with You as my light,
And I will stand strong because of Your might;
I will walk in the path You have set before me,
And I will not stumble because I can see;
Those things that may stand to hinder my view,
They are small and I will overcome because of You.

April 8

Psalm 119:145 "I cry out with my whole heart; Hear me, O Lord! I will keep Your statutes."

Each morning I rise to the glory of Your grace,
The beauty of the day reflecting Your face;
I speak to You and You hear my prayer;
The peace and joy in my heart tell me You are there;
To lead me and guide me through the day,
And You assure me as I walk in Your way.

April 9

Psalm 119:165 "Great peace have those who love Your law, And nothing causes them to stumble.

You are the righteousness of my peace,
The wonders of Your love will never cease;
To amaze me at the depth of Your care;
That Your law is simple and fair,
And that You will keep me upright today;
As I walk in the grace of Your way.

April 10

Psalm 121:1,2 "I will lift up my eyes to the hills–From whence comes my help? My help comes from the Lord, Who made heaven and earth."

No matter what this day may bring,
I will lift up my voice to You and sing;
And I will lift up my eyes to see Your face,
And I will praise You for Your mercy and grace;
The day was created for me to depend on You,
So You could show Your love as You see me through.

April 11

Psalm 127:1 "Unless the Lord builds the house, They labor in vain who build it; Unless the Lord guards the city, the watchman stays awake in vain."

You ,O Lord, are my master builder and guide,
There is nothing I can cover up or hide;
So as I build my life upon the goodness of Your grace,
Help my house be Your temple and resting place;
That it may be the refuge of those who suffer loss,
And I may be a watchman to lead them to the Cross.

April 12

Psalm 131:1 "Lord, my heart is not haughty, Nor my eyes lofty. Neither do I concern myself with great matters, Nor with things too profound for me."

I call upon You Lord to remind me of Your plan,
And not to be concerned with who I think I am;
But to remind me, that my heart belongs to You,
And that I am nothing, unless You see me through.
Life is greater than the distance I can see;
So let my concern be only of You in me.

April 13

Psalm 133:1 "Behold, how good and how pleasant it is For brethren to dwell together in unity."

As the day begins, let me be an example of Your call,
An example of unity in You and love for all;
Help me to dwell in the pleasant and the good;
And to walk in mercy as You would.
Hear me, Father, and those who call Your name;
That we may all be blessed walking without blame.

April 14

Psalm 139:23,24 "Search me, O God, and know my heart; Try me, and know my anxieties; And see if there is any wicked way in me, And lead me in the way everlasting."

When I wake each morning, draw my heart to You,
Call my name and search me through and through;
Because I desire to keep my heart pure and clean;
That Your way in me may be clearly seen;
Lead me in a way where anxieties are few,
For You created each day to be refreshing and new.

April 15

Psalm 145:21 "My mouth shall speak the praise of the Lord, And all flesh shall bless His holy name Forever and ever."

Each day the morning brings the praise of my heart,
To the One who created me and set me apart.
I will lift up my voice to my Lord in song;
To use this flesh for good and not for wrong;
I will bless Your name, my Lord and my King,
And through this flesh my spirit will sing.

April 16

1 Chron. 16:9 "Sing to Him, sing psalms to Him; Talk of all His wondrous works!"

Each day I wake to the sound of Your voice,
Calling in many ways through creations choice;
The sun sings to You with its' magnificent rays,
Reminding me of Your omnipotent ways;
Calling me to glorify You in the song I sing,
And praising You for the peace and joy You bring.

April 17

2 Chron. 15:7 "But you, be strong and do not let your hands be weak, for your work shall be rewarded!"

Keep me strong in Your works today, O Lord,
Help me show myself approved and in one accord,
With all that You have planned for me today;
That I may walk in the integrity of what I say;
And glorify You in the work of this land,
That all may see the glory of Your hand.

April 18

Job 5:8 "But as for me, I would seek God, And to God I would commit my cause."

For what reason would I not bring You my case,
To give my care to You and the mountain embrace?
For only You can see the future at hand,
And bring about victory and help me stand;
There is no other, but You to stand by my side;
And under Your wings is the place I'll hide.

April 19

Isaiah 1:18 "'Come now, and let us reason together,' Says the Lord,' Though your sins are like scarlet, They shall be as white as snow; Though they are red like crimson, they shall be as wool."

There is none like You to set me free,
And there is none like You who can see,
The joy in my heart of knowing Your are here;
And that I can live through the day without fear,
Because Your grace is beyond my reason to see;
Yet I know in my heart , Your love for me.

April 20

Hosea 2:20 "I will betroth you to Me in faithfulness, And you shall know the Lord."

You are the Husband, O Lord, and I am the bride,
I will be faithful and You will be by my side.
I will walk in integrity and in faith today,
Knowing that You will guide me along the way;
I will keep my eyes on You as I walk;
And will honor You to those whom I talk.

April 21

Joel 2:21 "Fear not, O land; Be glad and rejoice, For the Lord has done marvelous things!"

Each day I awake to the wonders that You do;
And realize how blessed I am to be part of You;
To know that I am safe in Your marvelous care;
And to know Your leading is a matter of prayer;
So I am glad and I will rejoice;
And will continue to listen for Your voice.

April 22

Micah 7:8 "Do not rejoice over me, my enemy; When I fall, I will arise; When I sit in darkness, The Lord will be a light to me."

There is nothing I could face today that would cause me to fear;
Because I know that You are my Lord and You are near,
And if I stumble You will be strong to help me stand,
Because I will walk the straight and follow Your command;
Trials will come, but fear will not be part,
Because of the presence of You in my heart.

April 23

Nahum 1:7 "The Lord is good, A stronghold in the day of trouble; And He knows those who trust in Him."

What a wonder You are that You would be my stronghold today;
That You would guide my steps along life's way,
That You know the love of my heart for You;
And You know that my trust is true.
There is no other Name that I would want to raise;
For only You are worthy of the glory and the praise.

April 24

Zephaniah 3:17 "The Lord your God in your midst, The Mighty One, will save; He will rejoice over you with gladness, He will quiet you with His love, He will rejoice over you with singing."

The sun comes up in the morning and I sing to You all the day long;
For You alone are worthy of my heart and my song;
You dwell in this home You call Your temple;
Though it is not perfect, but tattered and simple;
Yet You fill it with Your love, Your mercy, Your grace;
I will keep my eyes upon You and honor Your place.

April 25

Haggai 1:13 "Then Haggai, the Lord's messenger, spoke the Lord's message to the people, saying, 'I am with you, says the Lord.'"

I am listening for Your voice and I hear;
That You are with me, that You are near;
And I will not fail because You are my rock;
I will make it through the day no matter what the shock;
Because I hear Your voice, the whisper in my ear;
And there is nothing in this world that I should have to fear.

April 26

Malachi 3:17 "'They shall be Mine,' says the Lord of hosts,' On the day that I make them My jewels. And I will spare them As a man spares his own son who serves him.'"

I am so thankful that I belong to You alone,
And give thanks for the mercy and grace You've shown;
That I am Your creation, made by Your hand;
And have freedom to worship You in this land,
For there is no other Father who loves like You,
And no other Father who can give life anew.

April 27

Matt. 4:19 "Then He said to them,' Follow Me, and I will make you fishers of men.'"

This is the day that You have made and I will follow,
I will fill it with Your grace, a day not hollow;
That others made see Your love in me,
And come to know You, to be set free.
Make me a light for You, O Lord, today;
That I may draw to You in all that I say.

April 28

Mark 4:14 "The sower sows the word."

I will be a sower for You, O Lord, today,
And plant a seed to lead someone Your way;
How simple it is to make You my choice;
And long to hear the leading of Your voice.
Your Word is a promise on which I can depend;
And You are the Healer that leads a heart to mend.

April 29

John 1:3 "All things were made through Him, and without Him nothing was made that was made."

You are the Creator of only that which is real;
You are the one to Whom all things kneel;
Only You can bring peace to my soul;
And bring forth the beauty of a diamond from coal,
You have created this day for Your favor to me,
And I will praise Your name for all to see.

April 30

2 Cor. 2:14 "Now thanks be to God who always leads us in triumph in Christ, and through us diffuses the fragrance of His knowledge in every place."

You, O Lord, create each day to be a victory for me,
I must only trust in You and in Your strength must see,
The goodness of the day and honor You as I walk;
And for good things give You glory when I talk.
I will be what You have called me to today;
And will draw upon Your grace along the way.

May 1

Gal. 2:20 "I have been crucified with Christ; it is no longer I who live, but Christ lives in me; and the life which I now live in the flesh I live by faith in the Son of God, who loved me and gave Himself for me."

I know that I am no longer my own;
That You have lifted me up to share Your throne;
And created me anew to serve as Your hands;
To lift up Your name to all people and lands,
And though I live in the flesh on the earth,
I keep my eyes on my new kingdom berth.

May 2

Phil. 1:6 "Being confident of this very thing, that He who has begun a good work in you will complete it until the day of Jesus Christ."

Only by Your Spirit will my work become complete,
And only by Your power may I stand and not retreat;
Today I will move forward toward completion of Your call;
And listen to Your Spirits voice that keeps me from a fall;
I have begun the work that You have called me to;
And I will not fail because You will see me through.

May 3

1 Thess. 2:4 "But as we have been approved by God to be entrusted with the gospel, even so we speak, not as pleasing men, but God who tests our hearts."

Lord give me the boldness to speak as I should,
Not of my own accord, but as You would;
That others may hear the Gospel that is true;
A truth of life eternal in spite what some construe;
Help me be pleasing in Your eyes today, O Lord,
That my hands and my lips will speak of our accord.

May 4

1 Tim. 1:12 "And I thank Christ Jesus our Lord who has enabled me, because He counted me faithful, putting me into the ministry."

Each day that I wake, I wake to Your created things,
And look forward to what Your created day brings;
For You have called me to be Your work at hand,
To be an example to others in this land,
That I, as part of Your chosen kingdom,
May bring forth in You, Your people's freedom.

May 5

2 Tim. 1:12 "For this reason I also suffer these things; nevertheless I am not ashamed, for I know whom I have believed and am persuaded that He is able to keep what I have committed to Him until that Day."

There will be those who will call me bizarre,
Because I will acknowledge the King that You are,
But I will not be ashamed to call Jesus my King;
And will not be turned by what the day may bring;
For I have You in my heart, soul and mind;
No greater grace and love could I ever find.

May 6

Philemon 1:7 "For we have great joy and consolation in your love, because the hearts of the saints have been refreshed by you, brother."

I love You Lord, and Your love brings me great peace,
To know that Your love in me will never cease.
It brings joy that can't be explained in speech;
Yet brings understanding that all can reach.
For You are not far off as some might say,
But as close as my heart will let You stay.

May 7

Hebrews 1:3 "Who being the brightness of His glory and the express image of His person, and upholding all things by the word of His power, when He had by Himself purged our sins, sat down at the right hand of the Majesty on high."

You, Lord Jesus, are the Bright and Morning Star,
Created in me for who You are;
That Your power and glory would set my way;
To honor You and praise You as I bow to pray.
You have carried me too, to our Father on high,
To the grace of Your hand, none can deny.

May 8

1 Peter 1:7 "That the genuineness of your faith, being much more precious than gold that perishes, though it is tested by fire, may be found to praise, honor, and glory at the revelation of Jesus Christ."

Only You Lord, can see the truth of my praise;
Lifted up to You in a myriad of ways,
Not to boast, but to glorify Your name;
And to reveal to all the reason that You came;
While much on earth is given, a blessing to the land,
Only Jesus is eternal and the reason that I stand.

May 9

2 Peter 1:10 "Therefore, brethren, be even more diligent to make your call and election sure, for if you do these things you will never stumble."

I am strengthened by the certainty of Your grace,
I will admonish myself to stand rightly before Your face;
I will give myself to a diligent godly walk,
And to proper lips and righteous talk;
So I may be the person You called me to be;
And be worthy before You for all to see.

Spring

May 10

Isaiah 40:31 "But those who wait on the Lord Shall renew their strength; They shall mount up with wings like eagles, They shall run and not be weary, They shall walk and not faint."

Today is Your day, O Lord, I will not fail,
For You have made me the head Lord, and not the tail,
You have made me provision to rise on the wind;
To be assured my life You'll defend,
When I grow weary You'll renew my way;
And I'll overcome every trial today.

May 11

1 John 1:5 "This is the message which we have heard from Him and declare to you, that God is light and in Him is no darkness at all."

From sun up to sun up life's darkness can not stand,
For the light that You are emits the Father's hand;
The goodness of the Son lights up the darkest night;
And assures me of my throne regardless of my plight,
I will follow boldly and stand upon Your grace,
Until the light of heaven shines upon my face.

May 12

Proverbs 16:20 "He who heeds the word wisely will find good, And whoever trusts in the Lord, happy is he."

I will heed Your word, Lord, and find good,
Because I will walk in Your statutes as I should;
I will trust in You throughout the day,
And be careful for what my lips may say,
I will be happy as I walk this day through,
And give the praise for it all to You.

May 13

Proverbs 16:24 "Pleasant words are like a honeycomb, Sweetness to the soul and health to the bones."

Help me Lord be a vessel of sweet sounds,
Where Your mercy, grace, and love abounds,
That I may be a proven vessel in Your sight;
And bring forth an example of Your love and might.
You are the Master that brings about my healing;
You care about my body as well as my feeling.

May 14

2 John 1:6 "This is love, that we walk according to His commandments. This is His commandment, that as you have heard from the beginning, you should walk in it."

Your love, mercy, and grace for me abound;
Your commandments I keep, Your righteousness I've found;
I keep my ears open to hear Your word;
I will be a doer of what I have heard,
And I will walk according to what You say;
And receive Your blessings for me today.

May 15

3 John 2 "Beloved, I pray that you may prosper in all things and be in health, just as your soul prospers."

I thank You and praise You for Your love for me,
That You want me healthy, prosperous, and free,
I lift up my heart and sing with my voice,
To worship You for giving me a choice;
To walk out of darkness and into Your light;
To be precious and honorable in Your sight.

May 16

3 John 3 "For I rejoiced greatly when brethren came and testified of the truth that is in you, just as you walk in the truth."

Everyday I rejoice that You have given me a new day;
To walk in Your truth and in Your path stay,
Help me, Lord, be bold in my walk;
That good testimony comes as others talk;
I will rejoice when others see Your face;
I'll help them run a righteous race.

May 17

Jude 1,2 "To those who are called, sanctified by God the Father, and preserved in Jesus Christ: Mercy, peace, and love be multiplied to you."

I am called and sanctified and preserved by the Son,
Blessed by Jesus, the Holy and Anointed One;
Who knows who I am and calls me by name;
The Alpha and Omega Who always stays the same,
Your love is abundant in all that I do;
And Your grace sufficient to see me through.

May 18

Jude 20,21 "But you, beloved, building yourselves up on your most holy faith, praying in the Holy Spirit, keep yourselves in the love of God, looking for the mercy of our Lord Jesus Christ unto eternal life."

I will build my spirit by listening to Your Spirit;
Opening my mind and heart to hear it.
I will follow Your lead in all things;
And give You praise for the blessings that brings.
Holiness is what You long to see in me;
I will be Your example for all to see.

May 19

Jude 24,25 "Now to Him who is able to keep you from stumbling, And to present you faultless Before the presence of His glory with exceeding joy, To God our Savior, Who alone is wise, Be glory and majesty, Dominion and power, Both now and forever. Amen"

You, O Lord, are able to keep me from stumbling,
Your mercy and grace are both loving and humbling;
You stand before The Father to plead my case;
And stand beside me as I run my race;
You clear the mountains out of my way;
As I give You honor in my life today.

May 20

Leviticus 20:7 "Consecrate yourselves therefore and be holy, for I am the Lord your God."

You are my Lord and I am Your creation;
Not a figment of some vain imagination.
Therefore I will stand before You as holy;
By the blood of Your Son and in Him solely.
I will give myself to You and You alone;
As I run my race toward Your throne.

May 21

Rev. 1:3 "Blessed is he who reads and those who hear the words of this prophecy and keep those things which are written in it; for the time is near."

I will read and hear Your words, keep them and be blessed;
I will be Your example, in Your strength, I'll pass the test;
The signs of the end times are close at hand,
Wars and trials throughout the land;
But You, O Lord, are the keeper of my way;
And I will not fear for my life today.

May 22

Proverbs 31:28 "Her children rise up and call her blessed; Her husband also, and he praises her."

You are the Creator Who created a mother,
For a son, daughter, spouse there is no other;
A mother was created to show the Father's hand;
To be honored and blessed, that is His command;
To nurture and to guide with innocence of love;
To open children's hearts to the Father up above.

May 23

Rev. 1:8 "'I am the Alpha and the Omega, the Beginning and the End,' says the Lord, 'who is and who was and who is to come, the Almighty.'"

You are the beginning and the end of each day,
The cornerstone of all, along life's way;
You knew me before and will to the end;
On all things that come, on You I'll depend;
You are the one who all creation will seek;
And You are the grace that strengthens the weak.

May 24

Proverbs 3:27 "Do not withhold good from those to whom it is due, When it is in the power of your hand to do so."

Father, help me be the hands of giving and good;
That the power of Your love may be understood.
Let my power be of You in every good thing;
So the sound of Your grace and mercy will ring.
Only goodness and mercy comes from You;
Help my heart be pure in all that I do.

May 25

Rev. 2:26 "And he who overcomes, and keeps My works until the end, to him I will give power over the nation."

By Your word I will triumph in Your way;
And in Your power You will keep me today.
You will set my feet upon the rock of Your Son;
And by His name many will be won;
And all the nations will glorify His name;
And Your blessings on me and mine will remain.

May 26

Proverbs 4:7 "Wisdom is the principal thing; Therefore get wisdom. And in all your getting, get understanding."

Your word says that if I need wisdom, to ask;
So I ask for wisdom that I might complete each task.
I will be favorable in my journey for You ;
Understanding given will see me through,
And I will call upon Your name each day;
And will listen closely to what You say.

May 27

Proverbs 4:23 "Keep your heart with all diligence, For out of it spring the issues of life."

I will keep my heart pure, O Lord, before You;
And will dwell on those things that are true;
My life is open before all , with nothing to hide;
I pray all will see I dwell at Your side,
For the issues of life are only issues of call;
In You I will stand, I will not fall.

May 28

Proverbs 4:26 "Ponder the path of your feet, And let all your ways be established."

I will not take a step unless You are my guide;
For if You guide, I'll have nothing to hide.
Only You have the power to establish the day;
And only You have the grace to hear when I pray.
I will follow the path You set for me;
For today, as before, You have set me free.

May 29

Leviticus 20:7 "Consecrate yourselves therefore, and be holy, for I am the Lord your God."

Lord, this is Your day and You have made it well;
The glory of Your grace is what I must tell;
So give me the boldness to preach the Good News;
Your mercy and love, so it's You they will choose.
I will stand for You and walk the narrow path;
An example of Your love and not Your wrath.

May 30

Deut. 4:35 "To you it was shown, that you might know that the Lord Himself is God; there is none other besides Him."

Everyday when I wake I can see who You are;
I only have to open my eyes, You are not far;
Whether the day is cloudy or the sun shows its light;
Your creation and love has shown me Your might,
There is none other for Whom I want to live;
Today and always, my heart to You I give.

May 31

Joshua 1:9 "Have I not commanded you? Be strong and of good courage; do not be afraid, nor be dismayed, for the Lord your God is with you wherever you go."

Today is Your day and in it I will rejoice;
I will not be afraid or dismayed for I hear Your voice;
You call out grace that keeps me from all wrong;
You call out strength that keeps me walking strong,
So wherever I go and whatever I do;
I am not alone, Lord, I am with You.

June 1

1 Samuel 12:16 "Now therefore, stand and see this great thing which the Lord will do before your eyes."

I wake each morning to the sounds of Your creation;
And I see the stillness of the trees as if in meditation;
There branches lifted up as to praise Your name;
The mountains lifted high to glorify the same;
I stand each day to see the love that You show;
To all Your wonders You share here below.

June 2

2 Samuel 7:29 "Now therefore, let it please You to bless the house of Your servant, that it may continue before You forever; for You, O Lord God, have spoken it, and with Your blessing let the house of Your servant be blessed forever."

You alone are the Blessed One Who has spoken,
Blessings into being for the lonely and broken;
Because You know the heart of the lost;
Who You were willing to redeem at any cost,
So You gave Your only begotten Son;
That the broken and the lost including I might be won.

June 3

1 Chronicles 16:10 "Glory in His holy name; Let the hearts of those rejoice who seek the Lord!"

I will glory in Your name as I wake this day;
I will kneel before You, with honor I'll pray;
My heart will be lifted up as I praise Your name;
As I remember the reason why the Savior came;
I will rejoice in knowing the love You have for me;
And I will sing to You with joy for setting me free.

June 4

Job 5:17 Behold, happy is the man whom God corrects; Therefore do not despise the chastening of the Almighty."

I am happy that You lead me with a strong inner voice;
And correct me, in love, when I make a wrong choice;
I am happy that You love me enough to care;
And that my life is valuable enough to spare;
Therefore I do not despise Your Godly correction;
But praise You for the Spirit that leads to reflection.

June 5

Psalm 5:11 "But let all those rejoice who put their trust in You; Let them ever shout for joy, because You defend them; Let those also who love Your name Be joyful in You."

The start of my day starts with trust in You;
Because there is no other that can see me through,
My heart shouts a song and my voice will sing,
As I bask in the peace that Your blessings bring;
For there is no other who brings about such peace;
In whom compassion, mercy, and grace will never cease.

June 6

Proverbs 15:30 "The light of the eyes rejoices the heart, And a good report makes the bones healthy."

The light of Your eyes reflect in the sun,
And I rejoice in my heart knowing we are one;
Each day You create gives out a special call;
Your good report is that no one should fall;
That all should prosper and be in good health;
That all who walk righteous will share in Your wealth.

June 7

Ecclesiastes 3:1 "To everything there is a season, A time for every purpose under heaven."

Today You have called me to a glorious plan;
To overcome the challenge, to say that I can;
When I walk through the storm its just for a season;
I don't need to know the purpose or reason;
But just to know that in You I'll overcome;
For in every purpose and season, I know who I'm from.

June 8

Joel 2:32 "And it shall come to pass That whoever calls on the name of the Lord Shall be saved. For in Mount Zion and in Jerusalem there shall be deliverance, as the Lord has said, Among the remnant whom the Lord calls."

May this day bring a new revelation of You;
And may I touch many not just a few;
That each may feel the love of Your hand;
And realize the goodness of Your command;
That all may be delivered and follow Your way;
And that all will stand in Your grace today.

June 9

Haggai 2:4 "'Yet now be strong, Zerubbabel', says the Lord; 'and be strong, Joshua, son of Jehozadak', the high priest; and be strong, all you people of the land,' says the Lord,' and work; for I am with you', says the Lord of hosts."

What should I fear in this day, O Lord on high,
Knowing my strength is in You and You are nigh?
I will be strong and I will work with all haste;
I will redeem Your time and not let it waste.
You are the Lord who always makes the way;
And on Your word I can stand everyday.

June 10

John 1:4,5 "In Him was life, and the life was the light of men. And the light shines in the darkness, and the darkness did not comprehend it."

You are life, You are light, You are my all;
You are the reason I will not fall;
The light of You causes me to walk straight;
To have the strength to stand in the gate;
The darkness of the world can not stand;
Against the wonders You have planned.

June 11

Romans 1:17 "For in it the righteousness of God is revealed from faith to faith; as it is written, 'The just shall live by faith.'"

You have put me right with You, O Lord, justified;
Through faith in the Son who was crucified;
So that I could climb out of the pit of sin;
And by His very blood a guarantee to win;
To overcome the darkness the world sets to hide;
To overcome in truth by the Light I stand beside.

June 12

1 Cor. 1:18 "For the message of the Cross is foolishness to those who are perishing, but to us who are being saved it is the power of God."

The message of the Cross is the truth of life for me;
There is no other message that can set me free;
If only I believe, only then will I not perish,
The message of the Cross is a message I will cherish;
For only in You, my Lord, comes eternal grace;
Grace alone sufficient, till I look upon Your face.

June 13

2 Cor. 2:15 "For we are to God the fragrance of Christ among those who are being saved and among those who are perishing."

For me there is the sweet smell of salvation;
The wonder and the enjoyment of Your creation;
All things will stand before Your final throne;
And all things of Christ will finally be known;
For those who stand in You and for those who walk away;
There will be a time of judgement in that final day.

June 14

Colossians 2:6 "As you therefore have received Christ Jesus the Lord, so walk in Him."

The morning comes once again to the glory of Your praise;
I will walk in the honor of Your truth, Your banner raise;
I will keep my eyes firmly on the truth of Your call;
I will commit my life and give You my all;
For You are the power that keeps me straight and true;
And gives me total victory, when I keep my eyes on You.

June 15

2 Thess. 3:3 "But the Lord is faithful, who will establish you and guard you from the evil one."

Another day is coming, Lord, to show that You are faithful;
Help me Lord, to stand as bold, to show that I am grateful.
I can walk throughout the day, absent any fear;
Knowing You are by my side, standing always near;
To overcome the trials of life evil sends my way;
The armor of the Lord is strong, I put it on today.

June 16

Titus 3:5 "Not by works of righteousness which we have done, but according to His mercy He saved us, through the washing of regeneration and renewing of the Holy Spirit."

Nothing I can do today will make You love me more;
And only through Your grace , forget what's done before;
By the washing of the water, the Holy Spirit's lead;
And the mercy of the Lord and His word that I will heed;
Will I be accepted in the newness of my stand;
And reap eternal blessings by the goodness of Your hand.

June 17

Psalm 9:2 "I will be glad and rejoice in You; I will sing praise to Your name, O Most High."

I will be glad today and rejoice and worship Your name,
I will fill my day with gladness, being bold without shame;
I will lift my head high in proclaiming You are Lord;
And I will walk in Your way to receive the blessings stored;
For there is no other who can see me through;
There is no other God who loves me like You do.

June 18

Ecclesiastes 3:11 "He has made everything beautiful in its time. Also He has put eternity in their hearts, except that no one can find out the work that God does from beginning to end."

The day has been created and it is beautiful;
It is a day that calls me to be dutiful;
To the work of You that I love and cherish;
That all things in You may grow and not perish;
For there is no beginning or ending for me to find;
Only to keep Your love and grace entwined.

June 19

Jeremiah 10:12 "He has made the earth by His power, He has established the world by His wisdom, And has stretched out the heavens at His discretion."

All that has been and is, belong to the creation of Your hand,
And all of Your creation is blessed in the land;
For the power of Your heart brings me never ending grace;
And the power of Your love keeps my eyes upon Your face;
Help me stay upon the path that will bring me straight to You;
Give me strength and give me wisdom to stand for what is true.

June 20

Luke 6:38 "Give and it will be given to you: good measure, pressed down, shaken together, and running over will be put into your bosom. For with the same measure that you use, it will be measured back to you."

Your goodness is measured all the day long,
And I lift a grateful voice to You in song;
For You are the giver of more than I need;
Help me to stand against a worldly greed;
And to give of myself the gift of Your measure;
That I may receive the gift of Your pleasure.

June 21

John 1:16,17 "And of His fullness we have all received, and grace for grace. For the law was given through Moses, but grace and truth came through Jesus Christ."

I am blessed to be one who has received;
To be in the family of all who have believed;
Grace for me has come through His cost upon the tree;
No greater be the price than His call to set me free;
While the law was given, the greater is the Son;
Who through no greater love, our victory is won.

June 22

Proverbs 27:17 "As iron sharpens iron, So a man sharpens the countenance of his friend."

Lord, help me be a friend to someone in need today;
Help me lend a word that would lift them from the fray;
Help me lead them to the One who always stays the same;
And give the glory to the One who calls them by their name;
Help me be a leader, an example of Your call;
To help them see Your mercy and to keep them from the fall.

June 23

Prov. 27:19 "As in water face reflects face, So a man's heart reveals the man."

Lord, let my heart reveal the You in me;
A reflection that all may see;
That You are the love in this life You've granted;
And in it the seeds of grace You've planted;
That all may see more of Your reflection;
That reveals the truth of Your eternal protection.

June 24

1 Cor. 10:13 "No temptation has overtaken you except such as is common to man; but God is faithful, who will not allow you to be tempted beyond what you are able, but with the temptation will also make the way of escape, that you may be able to bear it."

I awake another day with confidence in You as my guide;
Knowing I am safe, if in You I will abide;
The tempter can come , but You will make the way;
And I will listen to Your voice and I will obey;
For You have given me victory over all to bear;
That I may be an example of Your love and care.

June 25

2 Cor. 4:6 "For it is God who commanded light to shine out of darkness, who has shone in our hearts to give the light of the knowledge of the glory of God in the face of Jesus Christ."

There is no other power that transcends the gift of all life;
No other love that can bring joy out of earthly strife;
For You commanded light to shine for me to see;
The light of the Son, Who has set me free;
All to the glory of Your Son full of grace;
Who shines His light of mercy upon this pilgrim's face.

June 26

Ephesians 2:8,9 "For by grace you have been saved through faith, and that not of yourselves; it is the gift of God, not of works, lest anyone should boast."

Lord, thank You for saving my soul,
And for Your care in making me whole;
To live an eternity in the glory of Your land;
To be forever safe by the grace of Your hand;
I know I am forever Yours, that is my gift;
And to Your praise, my heart I will lift.

June 27

Ephesians 2:10 "For we are His workmanship, created in Christ Jesus for good works, which God prepared beforehand that we should walk in them."

Lord, help me stand firm in Your love today,
Realizing I was created to be an example of Your way.
Created to be an example of the one and only King;
That all Your works in me would to Your glory bring;
For I know that I am nothing on my own;
Yet I know that with You in me I am not alone.

June 28

Colossians 3:1 "If then you were raised with Christ, seek those things which are above, where Christ is, sitting at the right hand of God."

Today I will seek those things above,
And in so doing will reap the benefit of Your love;
I can see You there at the Father's right hand;
As You guide Your sheep through this troubled land;
I will live by Your Spirit, the voice which I seek;
And I will follow Your voice whenever You speak.

June 29

2 Thess. 3:5 "Now may the Lord direct your hearts into the love of God and into the patience of Christ."

Direct my heart, O Lord, to be gracious today;
To walk in Your love, full of mercy along the way;
Father, help me to walk in the patience of Your Son;
And through that walk may many people be won;
May the light You have given show the path to sow;
And to those that are lost, the love of Jesus show.

June 30

Titus 3:8 "This is a faithful saying, and these things I want you to affirm constantly, that those who have believed in God should be careful to maintain good works. These things are good and profitable to men."

This is Your day Lord to affirm those who believe,
By my works I will be known and by Your grace I will receive;
The blessings that You promise for those who won't retreat;
May I glorify Your name in each trial that I may meet.
I will look to Your promise and the power of Your word;
And give You all the glory for good things that occurred.

July 1

Hebrews 4:12 "For the word of God is living and powerful, and sharper than any two-edged sword, piercing even to the division of soul and spirit, and of joints and marrow, and is a discerner of the thoughts and intents of the heart."

Search my heart today, O Lord, and call me to intent;
If there be impurity, lead me to repent;
For I want only, to stand before You pure;
To walk a path of righteousness, straight and sure.
May I be acceptable, may my walk be right;
And may my life give honor and be precious in Your sight.

July 2

James 5:16 "Confess your trespasses to one another, and pray for one another, that you may be healed. The effective, fervent prayer of a righteous man avails much."

Father, help me live righteous in your eyes today,
Help me lift my neighbor in things I say;
For those who need a touch, help me be Your light;
Help me be Your hands that portray Your grace and might.
The prayer of my lips will lift Your name on high;
And the mercy that You show, there is no way to deny.

July 3

1 Peter 5:8,9 "Be sober, be vigilant; because your adversary the devil walks about like a roaring lion, seeking whom he may devour. Resist him, steadfast in the faith, knowing that the same sufferings are experience by your brotherhood in the world."

Today is the day that You have created for me;
I will put on Your armor, I will not flee;
For the power of Your word strengthens my spirit;
And stands me strong each time I hear it.
I will not run from the adversary's roar;
For You are my shield that walks on before.

July 4

Hebrews 5:13,14 "For everyone who partakes only of milk is unskilled in the word of righteousness, for he is a babe. But solid food belongs to those who are of full age, that is, those who by reason of use have their senses exercised to discern both good and evil."

Each day brings a new revelation of the depth of Your grace,
And deepens my walk with You, from place to place;
I once was a babe, but now I strive to grow;
To mature in You in the things I need to know;
That I may be a doer of Your word day by day;
Skilled in discernment, a teacher of Your way.

July 5

2 Peter 3:14 "Therefore, beloved, looking forward to these things, be diligent to be found by Him in peace, without spot and blameless."

Each day when I wake I seek a day of peace,
Knowing that whatever comes Your grace will never cease;
And I will walk in You for righteousness sake;
Keeping Your light on the path that I take;
And I will leave the day secure in my case;
Looking to Your eyes and the smile upon Your face.

July 6

3 John 5,6 "Beloved, you do faithfully whatever you do for the brethren and for strangers, Who have borne witness of your love before the church. If you send them forward on their journey in a manner worthy of God, you will do well."

Lord, You are the witness that dwells within me,
Help me be that witness of You for all to see;
Help me be a light to lead others to Your hand;
Moving forward always to the Lord's command.
Call me to be graceful to all You send my way;
And on my journey faithful, that is what I pray.

July 7

Genesis 2:7 "And the Lord God formed man of the dust of the ground, and breathed into his nostrils the breath of life; and man became a living being."

Each day the sun shows itself new,
The light and the warmth remind me of You;
The glory of each day brings newness to live;
Newness in life which You abundantly give;
You are the Alpha and Omega, the beginning and end;
And even in all Your majesty, You call me Your friend.

July 8

Numbers 14:21 "But truly, as I live, all the earth shall be filled with the glory of the Lord."

The glory of Your presence is seen by my heart,
The vastness of Your grace I see only in part;
For each passing day brings new wonders to me;
The power of Your creation is a wonder to see;
But most of all, is the wonder of Your Son;
Whose love for me has made us one.

July 9

Proverbs 22:6 "Train up a child in the way he should go, And when he is old he will not depart from it."

Train me Lord, in the way I should go,
So that I may not be tossed to and fro;
And no matter how long a life You give;
I will grow in the way You want me to live;
That I may be an example as I walk through the day;
And receive the blessings as I listen and obey.

July 10

1 Samuel 12:24 "Only fear the Lord, and serve Him in truth with all your heart; for consider what great things He has done for you."

May the respect I have for You be evident in my walk,
That I serve none but You in action and talk;
Each day I consider the great things that You do;
The sunrise, the day, and sunset come from You.
What other or who could create such great things;
Than Your majesty of life and the joy it all brings.

July 11

2 Samuel 22:21 "The Lord rewarded me according to my righteousness; According to the cleanness of my hands He has recompensed me."

Every day You bless me beyond expected measure,
And remind me of Your grace and heavens waiting treasure;
For those who except and live, the truth before Your eyes;
And run the race of life, to win Your highest prize.
I will lift my heart and hands up toward Your face;
And stand upon Your word and the sureness of Your grace.

July 12

1 Chron. 16:29 "Give to the Lord the glory due His name; Bring an offering, and come before Him. Oh, worship the Lord in the beauty of holiness!"

I will give You the glory and honor due Your name,
My Lord never changing, Who always stays the same;
Who bares me up, when I'm tempted by it all;
In the face of the world You keep me from the fall.
I will bring You an offering, my heart to You I give;
And I'll give You the glory for the good this life may live.

July 13

Job 23:10,11 "But He knows the way that I take; When He has tested me, I shall come forth as gold. My foot has held fast to His steps; I have kept His way and not turned aside."

Only You, O Lord, know my heart, my soul, my mind,
And only in You will eternal treasures find;
I will stand fast, O Lord, in You I will abide;
There is nothing in my life that I will try to hide;
I will walk with You, O Lord, the path I know I should;
And when my time on earth is done, You'll see my heart as good.

July 14

Ecclesiastes 11:7 "Truly the light is sweet, And it is pleasant for the eyes to behold the sun."

I see the darkness and in light it disappears,
And with the coming of the light, disappears the fears;
For fears are present in the things that I can not see;
Comfort comes in knowing, that You are here with me;
And may the light of my life, be sweet upon Your face;
With the glow of all Your goodness and Your never ending grace.

July 15

Isaiah 6:8 "Also I heard the voice of the Lord, saying 'Whom shall I send, And who will go for Us?' Then I said, 'Here I am! Send me.'"

Each day that You give me Lord, I'll lift Your name on high,
In this land or in others, Your name I'll not deny;
I will go to a foreign land if You call me far away;
Or will be a light around me if You chose for me to stay;
However You may chose, I will listen and obey;
So call me Lord or send me Lord, I am willing day by day.

July 16

Lamentations 3:57 "You drew near on the day I called on You, And said, 'Do not fear!'"

Each day as I awake I can rely on Your presence of joy,
And stand firm against the devil's deceit and ploy;
When I draw near to You, on Your strength I can rely;
And stand on Your word when Your statutes I apply;
There is no reason for me to fear the world and hide,
For You are my Lord and always by my side.

July 17

Hosea 14:6 "His branches shall spread; His beauty shall be like an olive tree, And his fragrance like Lebanon."

Today Your light will spread around the land,
And all will know the power of Your hand;
The beauty of Your way is endless in time;
Poetry in motion from rhyme to rhyme;
That enters the heart with goodness and grace;
With the fragrance of sweetness filling each place.

July 18

Hosea 14:9 "Who is wise? Let him understand these things. Who is prudent? Let him know them. For the ways of the Lord are right; The righteous walk in them, But transgressors stumble in them."

Father, bless me with Your wisdom today,
That the goodness of You I may portray;
Walking wisely and understanding all things;
Receiving the blessings that obedience brings;
For I am not one who wishes to stumble;
But one wishing to walk both prudent and humble.

July 19

Haggai 2:9 'The glory of this latter temple shall be greater than the former,' says the Lord of hosts. 'And in this place I will give peace,' says the Lord of hosts."

I am Your temple Lord, and there is peace in me,
Peace that will show others how You've set me free;
May my heart be open for all with trial to enter;
And may You receive the glory, attention center;
For all those who seek out hope and grace,
May I be Your temple and gathering place.

July 20

Matthew 6:11 "Give us this day our daily bread."

There is never a doubt, in my heart, of Your provision,
Each day I follow Your way, is a wise decision;
And each day I look to You, You assure my way;
The bread You give is more than what I pray;
It is life beyond what any one could know;
It is grace eternal and the love You always show.

July 21

Luke 12:29,30 "And do not seek what you should eat or what you should drink, nor have an anxious mind. For all these things the nations of the world seek after, and your Father knows that you need these things."

Lord help me keep my mind in proper perspective,
And to Your promises faithful and receptive;
That I may seek proper things that never perish;
Those important things that I should cherish;
Your grace, hope, mercy, and love that never fade;
Receiving Your blessings because I have obeyed.

July 22

Luke 12:31,32 "But seek the kingdom of God, and all these things shall be added to you. Do not fear, little flock, for it is your Father's good pleasure to give you the kingdom."

When the day begins and I see the gifts You give,
Help me to understand the reason that I live;
To give honor to You for the life that You provide;
For all the good things You create, and from me you never hide.
It is Your pleasure to see my cup overflow;
It is also Your pleasure, in me for You to grow.

July 23

John 1:51 "And He said to him, 'Most assuredly, I say to you, hereafter you shall see heaven open, and the angels of God ascending and descending upon the Son of Man.'"

Lord, let my spirit be as open as that of Nathanael,
And my heart as devoted as that of Daniel;
That I may receive the angels of Your grace;
And feel the warmth and glow of heaven's place;
For every day that's given I will praise Your Holy Name;
Giving glory and thanksgiving that You always stay the same.

July 24

Acts 20:24 "But none of these things move me; nor do I count my life dear to myself, so that I may finish my race with joy, and the ministry which I received from the Lord Jesus, to testify to the gospel of the grace of God."

Lord, I have no fear for my life or what it may take,
To run the race of glory for the Gospel's sake;
For I run Lord with joy to finish the race;
To claim my prize and victory, to stand in Your grace;
Today I will continue to spread the Good News;
To be a light for others for the One they must choose.

July 25

Acts 20:28 "Therefore take heed to yourselves and to all the flock, among which the Holy Spirit has made you overseers, to shepherd the church of God which He purchased with His own blood."

Lord, lead me today to be an example for the flock;
To help lead them to You, the solid rock;
Help me be what You have called me to be;
A shepherd of Your church, called to oversee;
I ask the Holy Spirit to always be my guide;
To walk with grace and in Your love abide.

July 26

Acts 20:32 "So now brethren, I commend you to God and to the word of His grace, which is able to build you up and give you an inheritance among all those who are sanctified."

Lord, I am honored and humbled by Your love for me,
And thankful for Your grace that's set me free;
That I am sanctified in You day by day;
And that You lift me up as I travel in Your way;
Keep me on Your road as I turn my face to You;
I will give You glory for the good things that I do.

July 27

Acts 20:35 "I have shown you in every way, by laboring like this, that you must support the weak. And remember the words of the Lord Jesus, that He said, 'It is more blessed to give than to receive.'"

I am so blessed to be used as a blessing to others,
Help me today Father, to help my sisters and brothers;
Who may not be as fortunate as I to know You;
And who may not understand Your word as true.
Use me Lord to touch the heart of the weak of mind;
That I may be a light and in me You they'll find.

July 28

2 Cor.12:9 "And He said to me,'My grace is sufficient for you, for My strength is made perfect in weakness.' Therefore most gladly I will rather boast in my infirmities, that the power of Christ may rest upon me."

It is a blessing to know that You do not expect perfection,
But only that I receive the Son and believe in His resurrection.
I do not dwell in the areas where I am weak;
But I will lay them down and Your grace seek;
And I will repent to draw the power of Your grace;
And know Your goodness will advocate my case.

July 29

Galatians 6:8 "For he who sows to his flesh will of the flesh reap corruption, but he who sows to the Spirit will of the Spirit reap everlasting life."

As I begin my day I will set my eyes upon You,
And while I must live in this world and its view;
I will keep Your word before me along the way;
And will sow to Your Spirit and continually pray.
I will keep You at the center of my daily race;
And give You thanksgiving for your eternal grace.

July 30

1 Chron.16:34 "Oh, give thanks to the Lord, for He is good! For His mercy endures forever."

I give thanks and honor to You for being my God,
For walking with me in my daily trod;
For You are good and Your love endures forever;
Your mercy is free, not based on my endeavor;
I am created for Your purpose, a purpose of good;
So help me walk worthy Lord, as I should.

July 31

2 Timothy 4:7 "I have fought the good fight, I have finished the race, I have kept the faith."

The purpose of my life is to keep the faith and finish the race,
To keep my life in a proper place and my eyes upon Your face;
Being an example of Your Word to show the Gospel true;
That I may obtain the crown of eternal peace with You;
I will fight the good fight as I lift Your name in praise;
And walk along with You as You guide me through Your ways.

August 1

Psalm 7:10 "My defense is of God, Who saves the upright in heart."

Each day I lift my eyes toward the One who sits on high,
To the One whose love and mercy I cannot deny;
And no matter what trial may come my way;
Your grace and love will see me through the day;
For I need not look for any other shield;
You alone are the cover to which I yield.

August 2

Psalm 7:17 "I will praise the Lord according to His righteousness, And will sing praise to the name of the Lord Most High."

There is no other God but You that I will praise,
And to Your name a banner I will raise;
I will sing to You and glorify Your name;
Because Your love for me is why You came;
To be the righteous man I could not be;
To die and live again, to set me free.

August 3

Psalm 8:1 "O Lord, our Lord, How excellent is Your name in all the earth, Who have set Your glory above the heavens!"

O Lord how wonderful You are, so full of grace,
Lord of creation and the goodness in this place,
Your name is set on high over all the land;
Nothing is created except by Your hand;
For Your glory is seen as I live day by day;
As You mold my life like softened clay.

August 4

Psalm 9:1 "I will praise You, O Lord, with my whole heart; I will tell of all Your marvelous works."

The sun will rise today and I will praise You again,
Lifting up the Name of Jesus to all men;
My heart will sing the praises of His name;
The One who never changes, but stays the same;
The One who heals, the One of provision and grace;
To Him I will give honor and I will seek His face.

August 5

Psalm 9:10 "And those who know Your name will put their trust in You; For You, Lord, have not forsaken those who seek You."

What joy and peace Your promises bring,
Trust in You makes my heart sing;
For I know that You will never leave my side;
As I lift up my life and in You abide;
For each day I live it is You I will seek;
I will open up my heart and listen to You speak.

August 6

Psalm 13:5,6 "But I have trusted in Your mercy; My heart shall rejoice in Your salvation. I will sing to the Lord, Because He has dealt bountifully with me."

Thank You for Your grace and the mercy You give,
And for the everlasting life of peace I will live;
You have given to me abundance beyond thought;
A bountiful life to me You have brought;
What more could I give than to give what I am;
And to live my life in the image of the Lamb.

August 7

Psalm 16:8,9 "I have set the Lord always before me; Because He is at my right hand I shall not be moved. Therefore my heart is glad, and my glory rejoices; My flesh also will rest in hope."

I will set You before me in all that I do today;
And strive to be Your grace and compassion on display;
I will speak of Your goodness and the power of Your grace;
And will be an example to others in this place;
My heart will be glad and I will not retreat in fear;
For You, O Lord, are abiding near.

August 8

Psalm 16:11 "You will show me the path of life; In Your presence is fullness of joy; At Your right hand are pleasures forevermore."

Each step that I take will be on the narrow road;
The path of life by Your word You showed;
To my life You will bring the presence of light;
My walk will be steady and pleasing in Your sight;
You have shown me the way and the path I must walk;
In compassion I will live and in grace I will talk.

August 9

Psalm 17:3 "You have tested my heart; You have visited me in the night; You have tried me and have found nothing; I have purposed that my mouth shall not transgress."

When the day ends and it becomes night,
You will find that I am worthy in Your sight;
For I will speak Your honor in the day;
And no foul thing will deter my way;
Of living my life in honor of You;
Test my heart, O Lord, and find me true.

August 10

Psalm 20:4 "May He grant you according to your heart's desire, And fulfill all your purpose."

My heart's desire is to be pleasing in Your sight,
To feel Your presence and the glory of Your might;
To fulfill the glory and the honor of Your name;
To live a life that's worthy and void of any blame;
Fill me Lord with the blessing of my heart's desire,
To continue as Your servant with a heart on fire.

August 11

Psalm 18:32 "It is God who arms me with strength, And makes my way perfect."

Your path for me today has been properly planned out,
If I follow properly, the outcome is not in doubt;
For You have made a way for me to receive the best;
That I may overcome each trial and be greatly blessed.
It is You who give me strength to carry on the light;
To stand in perfection, to be righteous in Your sight.

August 12

Psalm 40:5 "Many, O Lord my God, are Your wonderful works Which You have done; And Your thoughts toward us Cannot be recounted to You in order; If I would declare and speak of them, They are more than can be numbered."

Today I will see the beauty of Your ways,
The wonders of Your works that never cease to amaze;
One after another, too many to declare;
Signs of Your majesty, that I may prepare;
To stand in Your light and the goodness of Your plan;
To give You the glory and the honor over man.

August 13

Psalm 46:4 "There is a river whose streams shall make glad the city of God, The holy place of the tabernacle of the Most High."

Lord, may the river of my heart stream forth the glory of You,
May this temple that You inhabit stand firm and true;
And be a city of gladness and goodness before all men;
That will show Your mercy and grace and turn them from sin.
Help me be a city that stands high on the hill;
That sends forth the message of Your love and Your will.

August 14

Daniel 5:14 "I have heard of you, that the Spirit of God is in You, and that light and understanding and excellent wisdom are found in you."

Father, like Daniel, let the integrity of my life speak good,
And help me be bold in You, as Daniel would;
Help me bring forth Your Spirit that lives inside;
So that all may know in me You reside;
Help my actions be tempered with wisdom and grace;
To encourage others to run with hope in their spiritual race.

August 15

Daniel 6:16 "So the king gave the command and they brought Daniel and cast him into the den of lions. But the king spoke, saying to Daniel, 'Your God, whom you serve continually, He will deliver you.'"

The world is full of traps and trials to bare,
Comfort comes from knowing You care;
I will serve You continually as You command;
And in Your strength I'll firmly stand;
No matter what trap or trial may come;
It's in Your strength my victory comes from.

August 16

Daniel 6:27 "He delivers and rescues, And He works signs and wonders In heaven and on earth, Who has delivered Daniel from the power of the lions."

You, O Lord , are the One who lifts me up,
You open the doors of heaven to fill up my cup;
Your signs and wonders are something to behold;
The truth of Your word is a message to be told.
I will be delivered as I travel through this day;
For You are the One who leads my way.

August 17

Daniel 9:4 "And I prayed to the Lord my God, and made confession, and said 'O Lord, great and awesome God, who keeps His covenant and mercy with those who love Him, and with those who keep His commandments.'"

Each morning I wake I confess a new day before You,
To keep my eyes on the God who sees me through;
Who keeps His promises to those who obey;
And keeps His covenant as I follow His way;
I will love You Lord with all my heart and soul;
And give You praise for keeping me whole.

August 18

Joel 2:26 "You shall eat in plenty and be satisfied, And praise the name of the Lord your God, Who has dealt wondrously with you; And My people shall never be put to shame."

Lord, You show Your love and great provision everyday,
I lift my voice and heart to You in thanksgiving as I pray;
I thank You for the shield of Your grace and love;
As You pour out Your blessings from up above;
I will never want because I belong to You;
And never fail because You will see me through.

August 19

Mark 14:38 "Watch and pray, lest you enter into temptation. The spirit indeed is willing, but the flesh is weak."

Father, help me today to keep my eyes on You,
To walk in Your light and to be faithful and true;
So many things will try to draw me away;
So help me stand strong in You today.
My spirit yearns to do Your will, my best;
Help me run straight and strong to pass each test.

August 20

Mark 16:16 "He who believes and is baptized will be saved; but he who does not believe will be condemned."

Lord, I believe and You can see the truth of my heart,
Believing is just the beginning of truth to impart;
Help me be an example of You today;
From baptism and living to the way I pray;
I am saved by the mercy and grace of Your hand;
And confirmed by the example of where I stand.

August 21

Acts 4:31 "And when they had prayed, the place where they were assembled together was shaken; and they were all filled with the Holy Spirit, and they spoke the word of God with boldness."

Lord as I gather with my friends today,
Give me boldness as to what I should say;
To glorify Your name in all that I do;
To begin the day and in it, follow You;
Let the boldness of my life be in it's proper place;
And each expression of You be seasoned with grace.

August 22

Acts 4:32 "Now the multitude of those who believed were of one heart and one soul; neither did anyone say that any of the things he possessed was his own, but they had all things in common."

Lord help me understand the grace of giving,
And the blessings that come from that kind of living;
Keep before me the power of Your mighty hand;
And that all things are created at Your command;
Help me be an example of things that are right;
And all who are lost see You as their light.

August 23

Acts 16:25,26 "But at midnight Paul and Silas were praying and singing hymns to God, and the prisoners were listening to them. Suddenly there was a great earthquake, so that the foundations of the prison were shaken; and immediately all the doors were opened and everyone's chains were loosed."

Father, when I feel down and imprisoned by the day,
Bring me remembrance that to You I can pray;
Each trial that comes I will know the end's in sight;
I will overcome it all, because You are my light;
I will lift up my voice and sing to You a song;
Because I know You love me and to You I belong.

August 24

Romans 8:28 "And we know that all things work together for good to those who love God, to those who are the called according to His purpose."

Lord I give You praise for Your call in me,
I give You honor for setting me free;
I thank You for the direction the Holy Spirit leads;
And for the goodness You show and supplying my needs;
Your purpose is clear as I walk in Your way;
And I honor Your call with my life today.

August 25

Romans 8:31 "What then shall we say to these things? If God is for us, who can be against us?"

The world has many trials and challenging things,
But it is comforting to know what my Father brings.
The power of Your way will bring about the victory;
Your word confirms it, from the beginning of history;
That nothing will stand against the goodness of Your call;
Nothing will prevail against me for You are my all in all.

August 26

Romans 8:37 "Yet in all these things we are more than conquerors through Him who loved us."

I will face the day with new strength to show,
Life in You who helps me to grow;
In all these trials that the world may bring;
Knowing I'm in You makes my heart sing;
For I cannot fail as we walk hand in hand;
For You are my power and the reason I stand.

August 27

Romans 8:38,39 "For I am persuaded that neither death nor life, nor angels nor principalities nor powers, nor things present nor things to come, nor height nor depth, nor any other created thing, shall be able to separate us from the love of God which is in Christ Jesus our Lord."

Everyday when I wake, my first thought is of You,
Of Your grace, mercy, and all things true;
For I am Yours, created by Your hand;
To follow Your grace and to follow Your command;
The joy of my heart sings to You Lord of grace;
Knowing I'll be with You when I finish my race.

August 28

Colossians 4:2 "Continue earnestly in prayer, being vigilant in it with thanksgiving."

Lord I give You my heart and lift my voice in prayer,
To give You praise for the way that You care;
Help me to be vigilant for those who may be lost;
To reach out with You at whatever the cost;
I give You praise for hearing my plea;
To touch through me to set them free.

August 29

Colossians 4:5 "Walk in wisdom toward those who are outside, redeeming the time."

Lord help me walk in humility toward others,
To lead them to You as my sisters and brothers;
Help me not be slack in the time I spend;
And to be a light for You in the message I send.
Give me grace Lord for all outside to see;
That they made recognize You in me.

August 30

Colossians 4:6 "Let your speech always be with grace, seasoned with salt, that you may know how you ought to answer each one."

Let the abundance of my heart be in my speech,
A light to those within my reach;
Help my actions be seasoned with grace;
And point to You no matter the place;
Lead me Holy Spirit in a proper way;
That I may lead others to Jesus today.

August 31

1 Chron. 29:12 "Both riches and honor come from You, And You reign over all. In Your hand is power and might; In Your hand it is to make great And to give strength to all."

Lord all that I have comes from Your power,
All that protects me comes from You, my strong tower;
All that I am that is good comes from Your lead;
Help me to use it to plant a proper seed.
While riches and honor may come my way;
I will give You the glory for I am Your clay.

September 1

1 Chron. 29:17 "I know also, my God, that You test the heart and have pleasure in uprightness. As for me, in the uprightness of my heart I have willingly offered all these things; and now with joy I have seen Your people, who are present here to offer willingly to You."

Test my heart today, O Lord, and have Your pleasure,
I pray that in my heart You will find Your treasure;
And that all in my life will be honorable before You;
That I might be a disciple held worthy and true;
For You search for a heart that is true and pure;
I pray You will find my walk bold and sure.

September 2

1 Timothy 1:14 "And the grace of our Lord was exceedingly abundant, with faith and love which are in Christ Jesus."

Your grace and mercy never cease to amaze me,
That You would lay down Your life and set me free;
Just so I could spend an eternity with You.
Even in this world Your blessings are not just a few;
But Your goodness pours out like water that's fresh;
And Your grace flows freely to abundantly bless.

September 3

Psalm 35:27 "Let them shout for joy and be glad, Who favor my righteous cause; And let them say continually, 'Let the Lord be magnified, Who has pleasure in the prosperity of His servant.'"

I will shout for joy because of Your favor,
And Your love and grace I will gladly savor;
For You have made me prosperous by Your hand;
You have given me abundance in the land;
And I will glorify Your name on high;
You have heard my plea, You have heard my cry.

September 4

Psalm 37:23,24 "The steps of a good man are ordered by the Lord, And He delights in his way. Though he fall, he shall not be utterly cast down; For the Lord upholds him with His hand."

My steps today are ordered by Your call,
And I will step boldly and stand tall;
For You, O Lord, are the One who guides my way;
And I will heed Your call of righteousness today;
For You will hold me up when I walk the unknown;
And someday I will boldly stand before Your throne.

September 5

Psalm 37:37 "Mark the blameless man, and observe the upright; For the future of that man is peace."

Lord I expect Your peace to follow my way,
For I will be blameless in my walk today;
Keep me before You as I walk a straight line;
That with respect I will be a proper sign;
To glorify in You and to secure my peace;
That my fellowship with You will never cease.

September 6

Psalm 37:40 "And the Lord shall help them and deliver them; He shall deliver them from the wicked, And save them, Because they trust in Him."

Lord thank You for delivering me from my trials,
Lifting me above all the worldly styles;
That come against what You would have me do;
For holding me up and seeing me through.
Your promise is more than I could ever ask;
And Your grace helps me overcome each task.

September 7

Psalm 38:9 "Lord, all my desire is before You; And my sighing is not hidden from You."

Lord there are days when I bow before the weight,
And it is hard for me walk true and straight;
But You know what I am and what I will be;
For I am Your temple, You live in me.
My sighs are not hidden, You know my heart;
Thank You Lord for the love You impart.

September 8

Psalm 40:9 "I have proclaimed the good news of righteousness In the great assembly; Indeed I do not restrain my lips, O Lord, You Yourself know."

The world around me is my great hall,
To pronounce the Good News and fulfill my call;
I will not falter or fail to lift Your name;
Your love for me is now and forever the same.
You alone know my desire for You is pure;
And with Your hand my walk will be sure.

September 9

Psalm 40:10 "I have not hidden Your righteousness within my heart; I have declared Your faithfulness and Your salvation; I have not concealed Your loving kindness and Your truth from the great assembly."

Each morning when I wake, I sing You a song,
Because I am sure to You I belong;
I will forever declare Your salvation;
And with Your mercy overcome temptation;
I'll give You glory for the kindness You show;
From my heart to my mouth, words of life will flow.

September 10

Psalm 41:12 "As for me, You uphold me in my integrity, And set me before Your face forever."

Lord help me live my life in the purity You seek,
And by the power of Your word my integrity speak;
For nothing will sway me from running my race;
To the highest prize of seeing Your face;
I will be Your light from the highest hill;
So help me walk in Your perfect will.

September 11

1 Corinthians 1:9 "God is faithful, by whom you were called into the fellowship of His Son, Jesus Christ our Lord."

I am called to the fellowship of Your Son,
And by His grace our victory is won;
For there is no other who I call Lord;
All who believe are in one accord;
That Jesus Christ has paid the price;
And by His blood His grace suffice.

September 12

1 Corinthians 2:12 "Now we have received, not the spirit of the world, but the Spirit who is from God, that we might know the things that have been freely given to us by God."

Worldly things are not what I prize,
The things of Your Spirit are before my eyes;
Help me understand Your gifts over gold;
And the things of this world will not gain their hold;
For the gift of Yourself is the greatest gift You could give;
And the promise of eternity where believers will live.

September 13

1 Corinthians 4:1 "Let a man so consider us, as servants of Christ and stewards of the mysteries of God."

Lord thank You for allowing me to be Your servant,
Help me maintain my call and be forever fervent;
To be a proper steward of the gifts of Your grace;
To give my life in all in presenting Your case;
Let all consider why, my life is calm with peace;
You are the same forever, Your love will never cease.

September 14

Psalm 46:4 "There is a river whose streams shall make glad the city of God, The holy place of the tabernacle of the Most High."

I am Your tabernacle, O Most High,
Your goodness and mercy I will not deny;
You Lord are the river that I forever seek,
The waters of life to strengthen the weak;
The weak become strong and Your city their place;
From You, streams of life and infinite grace.

September 15

Psalm 50:23 "Whoever offers praise glorifies Me; And to him who orders his conduct aright I will show the salvation of God."

You, O Lord, are worthy of glory and my praise,
Honor and truth to You I will raise;
May my life be pure and stand aright;
May I, in Your eyes, fight the good fight;
Hold me close as I lift up Your name;
Clothed in Your mercy, there is no blame.

September 16

Nahum 1:7 "The Lord is good, A stronghold in the day of trouble; And He knows those who trust in Him."

You are my stronghold and I trust in You,
In this day as in all, You will see me through;
Because You know my heart honors Your name;
I know my Creator and from where I came;
I will trust in You no matter what life may bring;
You bring me peace like a fresh running spring.

September 17

Nahum 2:1 "He who scatters has come up before your face. Man the fort! Watch the road! Strengthen your flanks! Fortify your power mightily.'"

The world tries to scatter my peace and take my joy,
But You, O Lord, have the answers to earthly ploy;
You are the warning voice that whispers in my ear;
You are the encouragement I always find so near;
I will man the fort, watch the road, strengthen my flanks;
And when the victory comes I will bow to You in thanks.

September 18

Habakkuk 2:2 "Then the Lord answered me and said: 'Write the vision, And make it plain on tablets, That he may run who reads it.'"

Lord, Your have made Your vision plain in Your word,
Help me to put into practice what I have read and heard;
Help me to run and not stumble on my way;
To listen closely and follow what You say;
I will run my race with full confidence in Your call;
And I will heed Your statutes and give You my all.

September 19

Habakkuk 2:4 "Behold the proud, His soul is not upright in him; But the just shall live by his faith."

Father, help me to put away any pride in my way,
Pride that would keep me from You today;
Help me focus my eyes on things of grace;
And not on things that the world may chase;
I will live in peace because my hope is in You;
And peace is surrounded by things that are true.

September 20

Habakkuk 3:17,18 "Though the fig tree may not blossom, Nor fruit be on the vines; Though the labor of the olive tree may fail, And the fields yield no food; Though the flock may be cut off from the fold, And there be no herd in the stalls—Yet I will rejoice in the Lord; I will joy in the God of my salvation."

Father, my Father, how wonderful You are to me,
That no matter the trial, Your goodness I can see;
Though the world may seem unyielding in it's pain;
To see You, the God of all salvation, is my gain;
No matter what the world may bring or what it may apply;
I will continue to rejoice in You and lift Your name on high.

September 21

Habakkuk 3:19 "The Lord God is my strength; He will make my feet like deer's feet, And He will make me walk on my high hills."

Lord You are my strength to endure,
You cause my step to be swift and sure;
You lift me up to the mountain top;
Your love and mercy nothing can stop;
All creation yearns to see the goodness of Your way;
I am filled with joy that You are with me today.

September 22

Zephaniah 2:11 "The Lord will be awesome to them, For He will reduce to nothing all the gods of the earth; People shall worship Him, Each one from his place, Indeed all the shores of the nations."

You are awesome to me and Father of all,
You are the only God to whom I will call;
I will worship You and call You my own;
I will be thankful when I stand before Your throne;
The earth may look to its own gods for peace;
But it's only in You that joy will never cease.

September 23

Zephaniah 3:17 "The Lord your God in your midst, The Mighty One, will save; He will rejoice over you with gladness, He will quiet you with His love, He will rejoice over you with singing."

What a delight You are as my heart reveals You to me,
So much goodness for all the world to see;
My heart sings and I know You rejoice;
Because in gladness I have made You my choice;
In times when life thunders in my ears,
You quiet me and sooth all my fears.

September 24

Proverbs 4:20-23 "My son, give attention to my words; Incline your ear to my sayings. Do not let them depart from your eyes; Keep them in the midst of your heart; For they are life to those who find them, And health to all their flesh."

I will heed Your word and follow Your way,
That I might be blessed by You today;
I will keep Your words and make my way pure;
And I will walk straight to make my way sure;
You are life and health to all the flesh;
And all that comes from You is pure and fresh.

September 25

Proverbs 8:34,35 "Blessed is the man who listens to me, Watching daily at my gates, Waiting at the posts of my doors, For whoever finds me finds life, And obtains favor from the Lord."

Lord, each day when I wake I look for You,
I look to Your word for what I should do;
I will stand at the gate and find You there;
I always find You when I seek You in prayer;
For You are life and full of grace;
For those who seek Your dwelling place.

September 26

Proverbs 12:15 "The way of a fool is right in his own eyes, But he who heeds counsel is wise."

Lord, help me be a person of grace and light,
Seeking Your counsel for what is right;
Steer me away from the heart of a fool;
Away from actions that may be cruel;
Open my eyes and my heart to Your way;
That I may be wise in Your eyes today.

September 27

Proverbs 12:18 "There is one who speaks like the piercing of a sword, But the tongue of the wise promotes health."

Lord, help my words be seasoned with salt,
Help me speak softly and wisely as I ought;
That I might be a voice of peace and calm;
And for the human spirit a healing balm;
Let the words that I say show glory to the King;
And to the lost Your salvation bring.

September 28

Proverbs 14:29 "He who is slow to wrath has great understanding, But he who is impulsive exalts folly."

Each day that I wake up is opportunity to see,
The greatness of You that resides in me;
For my lips are mine, but You are my guide;
Let every word that I speak not be words to hide;
Let not my words be those demanding;
But words of mercy and understanding.

September 29

Proverbs 15:1 "A soft answer turns away wrath, But a harsh word stirs up anger."

Lord remind me of Your words as I walk through the day,
And help me speak grace in all that I say;
Help me respond to harshness by being kind;
And receive all comments with an open mind;
Help my speech impart a humble life;
That I'll not be the cause of anger or strife.

September 30

Proverbs 16:3 "Commit your works to the Lord, And your thoughts will be established."

I will commit my way to You today,
And ask the Holy Spirit to guide my way;
Help me today to finish my task;
To follow Your guide and do what You ask.
My thoughts are to establish the works of Your hand;
And to finish the work that You have planned.

October 1

Proverbs 17:9 "He who covers a transgression seeks love, But he who repeats a matter separates friends."

Lord help me be like You and treat my friends with care,
And when they stumble or fall, cover them in prayer;
Help me be wise counsel when there is a need;
That I may be the light of You and plant a proper seed;
To walk in love and understand how my friend may feel;
Help me guard my heart, O Lord, and choose a word to heal.

October 2

Proverbs 19:11 "The discretion of a man makes him slow to anger, And his glory is to overlook a transgression."

Lord let Your joy in me overtake a wrong that's done,
And mercy, grace prevail by the power of the Son,
Let all grace be seasoned in the willingness to forgive;
And in repentant hearts that change the life they live;
Guard my heart, O Lord, that I may be a light;
The glory of Your heart and steadfast in Your sight.

October 3

Proverbs 20:11 "Even a child is known by his deeds, Whether what he does is pure and right."

Father, lead me in every action toward a rightful deed,
I give You all the glory as You meet my every need;
Let me see Your goodness and open up my sight;
And I will give You honor for leading me to right;
I am Your child and reflect upon Your way;
Help me be a light that plants a seed today.

October 4

Proverbs 20:27 "The spirit of a man is the lamp of the Lord, Searching all the inner depths of his heart."

Lord, it is a new day and I will be Your lamp,
I will be the light that shines for my Savior's camp;
Search my heart Lord and find it pure;
Your temple walking straight and sure;
Each day I pray I'll heed Your call;
To give You my life, to give You my all.

October 5

Proverbs 22:4 "By humility and the fear of the Lord Are riches and honor and life."

There is no greater honor than to call You Lord,
For us to dwell together and live in one accord;
In You are the riches of eternal living;
Only in You Lord I have the gift of giving;
In humility is honor, mercy, grace;
Giving me the strength to run a worthy race.

October 6

Proverbs 24:19,20 "Do not fret because of evildoers, Nor be envious of the wicked; For there will be no prospect for the evil man; The lamp of the wicked will be put out."

Father, help me to stand firm in the way that is right,
For I am in Your protection, whatever the plight;
Evil may appear to prosper in its way;
But prosperity is fleeting and will end in that day;
When You come O Lord and shine Your light upon the land;
And the evil and the lost will be vanquished by Your hand.

October 7

Proverbs 25:26 "A righteous man who falters before the wicked Is like a murky spring and a polluted well."

Father, help me keep steady with my eyes on You,
Keep me from faltering and my perspective true;
I will not let the world or its ways blur my vision;
Nor let those around me cause spiritual division;
Keep me clean and my walk before You pure;
With You as my focus and with steps steady and sure.

October 8

Proverbs 27:19 "As in water face reflects face, So a man's heart reveals the man."

I know that what I do today reflects who I am,
Am I filled with grace as the Shepherd for the lamb?
Is my heart in the place that it needs to be;
And am I a reflection of what You see in me?
I pray that my behavior reflects a greatful heart;
At the end of the day, as well as from the start.

October 9

Proverbs 28:13 "He who covers his sins will not prosper. But whoever confesses and forsakes them will have mercy."

Father help me not take Your grace for granted,
And in my heart understand the truth that You have planted,
That by my Savior's blood You have set me free,
And by my choice I can show that You dwell in me.
You tell me in Your Word that I can have the best,
If in Your Word I'll dwell and if in You I'll rest.

October 10

Proverbs 30:5 "Every word of God is pure; He is a shield to those who put their trust in Him."

Lord, I give You praise that I can stand on what You say,
That Your word is sufficient for what may come today;
I am covered by Your shield of presence and purity;
The victory of life You have given is a surety;
You are the shield and I am covered by Your hand;
I will not be dismayed and on Your word I will stand.

October 11

Proverbs 30:8,9 "Remove falsehoods and lies far from me; Give me neither poverty nor riches—Feed me with food allotted to me; Lest I be full and deny You, And say 'Who is the Lord?' Or lest I be poor and steal, And profane the name of my God."

Father, let not the world deceive me into pride,
Into thinking life is full without You by my side;
Remind me daily that You fill my every need;
And when those needs are filled help me take heed;
To understand Your provision as a blessing of grace;
Not something worldly that can take Your place.

October 12

Ecclesiastes 3:1 "To everything there is a season, A time for every purpose under heaven."

Father, I do not always understand Your reason,
But help me trust in You no matter the season;
Help me understand there is purpose in it all;
And the purpose for me is to trust in Your call.
I will not concern myself with things I can't control;
And even in the trial I will give You my extol.

October 13

Ecclesiastes 3:14 "I know that whatever God does, It shall be forever. Nothing can be added to it, And nothing taken from it. God does it, that men should fear before Him."

Everything created is created for Your pleasure,
And everything created is created without measure;
And what has been created was created in perfection;
For joy in Your fellowship as we follow Your direction;
There is nothing man can add and nothing take away;
Help me be thankful for what I have today.

October 14

Ecclesiastes 4:9,10 "Two are better than one, Because they have a good reward for their labor. For if they fall, one will lift up his companion. But woe to him who is alone when he falls, For he has no one to help him up."

In the beginning You saw it was not good to be alone,
That each of us could not be complete on our own;
Your creation contained a pair of every kind;
That each one may, a like companion find;
To share in all that life has to give;
And to lift each other up in the life we live.

October 15

Isaiah 1:19 "If you are willing and obedient, You shall eat the good of the land."

Lord, help me hear Your will for me today,
And to be obedient to what You have to say;
I am willing and will be obedient to Your call;
Search my heart, O Lord, keep me from a fall;
I will receive today, the promise of Your good;
Because You are my strength and I'll walk as I should.

October 16

Isaiah 5:20 "Woe to those who call evil good, and good evil; Who put darkness for light, and light for darkness; Who put bitter for sweet and sweet for bitter!"

Lord, there are those who are deceivers to my ear,
That call things as they see them and not as they appear;
Help me stand firm in what is written by Your hand;
Not by the values forever changing in this land;
Help me not be deceived into thinking all is lost;
No matter what the world may say, my Savior paid the cost.

October 17

Isaiah 6:8 "Also I heard the voice of the Lord saying, 'Whom shall I send, And who will go for Us?' Then I said, 'Here am I! Send me.'"

Lord, Your call is to live a life of service to mankind,
That all will come to know You and none be left behind;
So help me be the light You have called me to be;
That I might lead others to You and set them free;
You have called and said, who will spread My word;
And I will answer the call to those who have not heard.

October 18

Isaiah 7:14 "Therefore the Lord Himself will give you a sign: Behold, the virgin shall conceive and bear a Son, and shall call His name Immanuel."

Immanuel, God with us, is the sign of which You speak,
Then a sign of hope, for the Savior which I seek;
Jesus now has come and lives within my heart;
Worthy of all praise and to others to impart;
Jesus Christ above all names in victory set me free;
To live my life to be Your light for the lost to see.

October 19

Isaiah 9:2 "The people who walked in darkness Have seen a great light; Those who dwelt in the land of the shadow of death, Upon them a light has shined."

Lord, I once walked in darkness never hearing Your voice,
But then You came to be my light giving me a choice;
From darkness and death to light and life I came;
The blood of my Savior took away my blame;
Help me Lord continue, good news of eternal reign;
Filling of all life with hope and victory over pain.

October 20

Isaiah 12:1 "And in that day you will say: 'O Lord, I will praise You; Though You were angry with me, Your anger is turned away, and You comfort me.'"

Thank You for Your Son, who turned away Your anger,
To be part of Your family, Now no longer a stranger;
You have given me comfort as I walk in Your way;
And give me strength as I follow You today;
I will praise You always with all that is within;
And thank You Lord, for redeeming me from sin.

October 21

Isaiah 12:2 "Behold, God is my salvation, I will trust and not be afraid; For Yah, the Lord, is my strength and song; He also has become my salvation."

I will trust in You today, Lord, as I always do,
I stand on Your word because I know it's true;
There is nothing in the day or night that should cause me fear;
In my heart I know that You are always near;
I can feel Your presence alive and well in me;
You have given me Your Spirit to be what I can be.

October 22

Isaiah 12:5,6 "Sing to the Lord, for He has done excellent things; This is known in all the earth. Cry out and shout, O inhabitant of Zion, For great is the Holy One of Israel in your midst!"

I will sing to You for You, O Lord, are worthy of my praise,
I will lift up my voice to You for the rest of my days;
For You have made me whole and part of Your Kingdom reign;
The glory of Your Son on High the Good News message plain;
No one can deny grace and power in the Son;
The blood upon the Cross that made believers one.

October 23

Isaiah 13:4 "The noise of a multitude in the mountains, Like that of many people! A tumultuous noise of the kingdoms of nations gathered together! The Lord of hosts musters The army for battle."

My voice gathers with many as I lift up my voice in praise,
For we who are believers stand together in these days;
To band and stand together to pray and lift ovations;
And to come together as one no matter what our nations;
For You, O Lord, are glory, our victory has been won;
Your people see Your mercy and the wonder of Your Son.

October 24

Isaiah 25:1 "O Lord, You are my God. I will exalt You, I will praise Your name, For You have done wonderful things; Your counsel of old are faithfulness and truth."

Each morning when I wake, I look for something new,
The glory of the sun I see, its warmth reminds of You;
I will seek Your counsel, truth, and faithfulness of old;
I will listen with my whole heart and do what I am told;
Living by example I will lift and praise Your name;
Father, Son, and Holy Ghost forever more the same.

October 25

Isaiah 26:7 "The way of the just is uprightness; O Most Upright, You weigh the path of the just."

Lord, You seek out those who walk in a righteous way,
Who walk justly and do just what You say;
You are the judge of those who walk upright;
Your promises affirmed for those precious in Your sight;
You show favor and grace to the just who've believed;
And are praised for the blessings and love that's received.

October 26

Isaiah 26:12 "Lord, You will establish peace for us, For You have also done all our works in us."

Father, You are the peace established in me,
Given by grace to set me free;
To do Your good works by dwelling inside;
My strength in You, takes away all my pride;
Thank You Lord for establishing my way;
For being my Lord and guiding me today.

October 27

Isaiah 33:15,16 "He who walks righteously and speaks uprightly, He who despises the gain of oppressions, Who gestures with his hands, refusing bribes, Who stops his ears from hearing of bloodshed, And shuts his eyes from seeing evil; He will dwell on high; His place of defense will be the fortress of rocks; Bread will be given him, His water will be sure."

Father, I am Your servant and I will be Your light,
I will strive to be one righteous in Your sight;
I will be Your hands that refrain from evil will;
And stand in Your strength against evils that kill;
For You are the power that dwells in me;
And provision sure for all to see.

October 28

Isaiah 35:3,4 "Strengthen the weak hands, And make firm the feeble knees. Say to those who are fearful-hearted, "Be strong, do not fear! Behold, your God will come with vengeance, With the recompense of God; He will come and save you."

The power of Your word is my promise to prevail,
With You by my side it is impossible to fail;
I will not be weak hearted and fall to fear;
For You are in my heart and always near;
The trial may come, but the battle is a sign;
That You will be my shield and the victory is mine.

October 29

Isaiah 35:8 "A highway shall be there, and a road, And it shall be called the Highway of Holiness. The unclean shall not pass over it, But it shall be for others. Whoever walks the road although a fool, Shall not go astray.

The hope of life is only You,
In life's long road You'll see me through;
You have made the road straight for me to travel;
And though the world may block with rock and gravel;
You light my way so I can see;
The wonder of life You have created for me.

October 30

Isaiah 64:8 "But now, O Lord, You are our Father; We are the clay, and You our potter; And all we are the work of Your hand."

Father, where You call I'll go,
The precious love of Christ to show;
To use a humble man like me;
To touch a heart and set it free;
The Good News story to one more told.
To bring one spirit into the fold.

October 31

John 14:6 "Jesus said to them, 'I am the way, the truth, and the life. No one comes to the Father except through Me.'"

In this day Your name will be lifted on high,
Jesus, the Son of God I will not deny;
There is only one way to the throne of grace;
To kneel at the Cross where He took my place;
No matter what this day may bring;
I will call You Lord, my Savior, my King.

November 1

Isaiah 44:6 "Thus says the Lord, the King of Israel, And His Redeemer, the Lord of hosts: I am the First and I am the Last; Besides Me there is no God."

There is no other who can redeem my spirit man;
You are the First and Last, the only God who can.
Others may come and falsely claim a place;
But they will be revealed in each and every case;
All will see the one true God who was from the beginning;
In truth the Savior who has come to save us from our sinning.

November 2

Isaiah 44:24 "Thus says the Lord, your Redeemer, And He who formed you from the womb: 'I am the Lord, who makes all things, Who stretches out the heavens all alone, Who spreads abroad the earth by Myself."

Each morning reveals to me the power of Your hand,
You're the center of my grace and the reason I can stand;
Each day You create the rays of warmth that feed;
And the beauty of Your land growing from a seed;
More than that, You came to be life's eternal light;
To love me just the way I am and save me from my plight.

November 3

Isaiah 45:3 "I will give you the treasures of darkness And hidden riches of secret places, That you may know that I, the Lord, Who call you by name, Am the God of Israel."

Lord, there are many things hidden that I cannot see,
But I know that You have treasures waiting here for me;
The world hides them in darkness, but You will be my light;
And as I seek Your righteous way they'll show up in my sight;
The greatest treasure I can have is that You know my name;
And that in love, You sent Your Son to carry all my blame.

November 4

Isaiah 48:17 "Thus says the Lord, your Redeemer, The Holy One of Israel: I am the Lord your God, Who teaches you to profit, Who leads you by the way you should go.'"

Lord, if I will listen, You will lead the way,
You are the One who provides for me today;
I will give You all the honor and lift Your name up high;
For all the blessings given and the sorrow passing by;
You save me in the trials and point me where to go;
You teach me through Your grace and show me how to grow.

November 5

Psalm 111:1,2 "I will praise the Lord with my whole heart, In the assembly of the upright and in the congregation. The works of the Lord are great, Studied by all who have pleasure in them."

Father, create in me a heart to see,
The love You have for others and me;
To heed Your call upon my life;
To be a light for others in strife;
That I may yield to Your will today;
To lead others to Your love and to Your way.

November 6

Galatians 5:1 "Stand fast therefore in the liberty by which Christ has made us free, and do not be entangled again with a yoke of bondage."

Help my heart lead others to Your face,
To see their loss, without Your grace;
Help me lift, to all, Your name;
One who never changes and remains the same;
Help me be Your love and light they see;
A seed of life to set them free.

November 7

Psalm 112:1,2 "Blessed is the man who fears the Lord, Who delights greatly in His commandments. His descendants will be mighty on earth; The generation of the upright will be blessed."

Father, You are my Lord and I delight in Your way,
I am blessed and thankful I can stand on what You say;
My children will be blessed as they honor Your command;
A generation of light and bold in their stand;
Your power and strength is my shield;
In You I will stand and to You I will yield.

November 8

Psalm 113:7,8 "He raises the poor out of the dust, And lifts the needy out of the ash heap, That He may seat him with princes— With the princes of His people."

Father, I came from the dust and have been set on high,
By the power of Your Son who has heard my cry;
I am one in Your family, lifted from the heap;
To live by Your light and Your promises keep;
By Your grace I've been lifted with the King of Kings;
To sit at Your right hand where the multitude sings.

November 9

Psalm 116:1,2 "I love the Lord, because He has heard My voice and my supplications. Because He has inclined His ear to me, Therefore I will call upon Him as long as I live."

I love You Lord, You never cease to hear,
To calm me in trial and take away my fear;
You have inclined Your ear and covered me with grace;
I will live my life for You in this earthly race;
I will call upon Your name with honor and with praise;
And thank You that You walk with me till the end of days.

November 10

Psalm 119:9 "How can a young man cleanse his way? By taking heed according to Your word."

Father, each day brings a newness of life,
Goodness and grace and suffering and strife;
But You, O Lord, are the victory of the day;
Giving comfort and love, come what may;
Help me keep my way clean before Your throne;
Heeding Your Word and proper seeds being sown.

November 11

Psalm 119:36,37 "Incline my heart to Your testimonies, And not to covetousness. Turn away my eyes from looking at worthless things, And revive me in Your way."

My want is not worthy unless it is of You,
I will listen to Your words because I know they're true;
I will not wish for another person's treasure;
But trust in You for my own life's measure;
Keep my eyes focused on eternity's gain;
And looking away from earthly bane.

November 12

Psalm 122:1 "I was glad when they said to me, 'Let us go into the house of the Lord.'"

Father, I will enter Your house with praise and thanksgiving,
Each day I will remember You, Your good reliving;
Your house will be a house of praise for all who seek;
A house where the strong will shepherd the weak;
A house where the love of You stands tall;
A house where to You I commit my all.

November 13

Psalm 122:7,8 "Peace be within your walls, Prosperity within your palaces. For the sake of my brethren and companions, I will now say, 'Peace be within you.'"

I will seek You today to claim my peace,
And thank You that Your love will never cease;
That prosperity follows the righteous of hand;
With provision of blessing upon the land;
I walk in peace because You are my Lord,
And with all people, pursue one accord.

November 14

Psalm 125:1 "Those who trust in the Lord Are like Mount Zion, Which cannot be moved, but abides forever."

I will stand upon the high place where I can see;
And dwell in the love that You have for me;
I will not be moved by man from my place;
But will stand on Your promises and live in Your grace.
You are the shield that guards my way;
I will give You honor and praise today.

November 15

Psalm 125:4 "Do good, O Lord, to those who are good, And to those who are upright in their hearts."

I will follow Your good with an upright heart,
I will be a light and will do my part;
To lead the lost toward Your grace;
Darkness to light and to Your dwelling place.
With Your strength I will be a house of good;
A candle of the Lord where darkness once stood.

November 16

Psalm 128:1,2 "Blessed is everyone who fears the Lord, Who walks in His ways. When you eat the labor of your hands, You shall be happy, and it shall be well with you."

Lord, thank You for the blessings on the way,
I can believe and stand on what You say;
The labor of my hands is not labor of loss;
But labor of love, results of the Cross;
I will be happy with Your Spirit the key;
For greater is the Holy One living in me.

November 17

Psalm 130:3,4 "If You, Lord, should mark iniquities, O Lord, who could stand? But there is forgiveness with You, That You may be feared."

There is forgiveness in You, that You may be feared,
In the sending of Your Son, my sins were cleared;
For I can stand on nothing of my own;
But by the death of the Son, mercy was shown;
Then He lives again to redeem me to You;
And send the Holy Spirit to see me through.

November 18

Hebrews 13:1,2 "Let brotherly love continue. Do not forget to entertain strangers, for by so doing some have unwittingly entertained angels."

Father, help me to lift my heart toward those not known,
That I may understand that I am not my own;
But that You have called me to be Your light;
For others to see and gain their sight;
That they may see Your love in me;
And this sign of You will set them free.

November 19

Psalm 133:1 "Behold, how good and how pleasant it is, For brethren to dwell together in unity!"

Lord, Your desire is for us to live in unity as one,
That Your will on earth might be done;
For brothers and sisters, in You, to be a light;
So in the eyes of others it is a pleasant sight;
For I am to be an example of honor for You;
That others may see the one God that's true.

November 20

Psalm 138:1,2 "I will praise You with my whole heart; Before the gods I will sing praises to You. I will worship toward Your holy temple, And praise Your name For Your loving kindness and Your truth."

I honor You, O Lord, by the way I live,
I lift my hands to praise what You give;
I will sing to You and lift up Your name;
Your kindness and truth remain the same;
Let all things as idols be cast far from me;
Help me dwell on what You want me to be.

November 21

Matthew 9:37,38 "Then He said to His disciples, 'The harvest truly is plentiful, but the laborers are few. Therefore pray the Lord of the harvest to send out laborers into His harvest.'"

Father there are those who are ripe in the field,
Send me to lead them, to You I will yield;
I will be Your laborer to send their way;
A worker in the harvest to teach them to pray;
All the glory will be lifted up to You;
As one by one they come, yielded and true.

November 22

Colossians 2:6,7 "As you therefore have received Christ Jesus the Lord, so walk in Him, rooted and built up in Him and established in the faith, as you have been taught, abounding in it with thanksgiving."

I am in You and abounding in Your grace,
Lord of the harvest You have shown me Your face;
I will walk with You yielding as I am taught;
Abounding in truth and rooted as I ought;
So I may live with thanksgiving as my praise;
Living built up and established in Your ways.

November 23

Jeremiah 1:17 "Therefore prepare yourself and arise, And speak to them all that I command you. Do not be dismayed before their faces, Lest I dismay you before them."

Father, I prepare myself daily to arise and go,
For there are so many that need to know;
While trials may come I will not be dismayed;
And will in Your presence, not be afraid;
Nor will I show others concern or fear;
For You, O Lord, are always near.

November 24

Jeremiah 2:11 "Has a nation changed its gods, Which are not gods? But My people have changed their Glory for what does not profit."

Lord, look around me and tell me what to do,
Has my nation changed its love for You?
Is all done for profit and lust;
Look in me Lord, have I lost my trust?
Lord, help me to see the direction to take;
To stand strong in You and Your Word not forsake.

November 25

Jeremiah 3:22 "Return you backsliding children, And I will heal your backslidings, Indeed we do come to You, For You are the Lord our God."

Father, examine my heart toward Your rule,
And remind me, Lord, that I am Your tool;
To help those who have lost their way, return;
Give them a new heart which for You, will yearn;
There is no other God to prepare their way;
You are the only God that can hear us pray.

November 26

Jeremiah 4:22 "For my people are foolish, They have not known Me. They are silly children, And they have no understanding, They are wise to do evil, But to do good they have no knowledge."

Father, know my heart and that I am true,
I have understanding and am part of You;
I have not turned away to foolish things;
But am standing firm in what Your blessing brings;
You have given me knowledge and made me right;
Help me to walk worthy and precious in Your sight.

November 27

Malachi 3:12 "'And all nations will call you blessed, For you will be a delightful land,' Says the Lord of hosts."

I have not left You and will always call You Lord,
I will pray for my land that we may live in one accord;
That we may be delightful in Your eyes;
A land of the Spirit without compromise;
All nations will see the blessings of Your hand;
And lift up Your name as God of their land.

November 28

Psalm 139:1 "O Lord, You have searched me and known me. You know my sitting down and my rising up; You understand my thoughts afar off."

Lord, You are Creator and know my every thought,
Your word leads and guides and by Your Spirit I am taught;
You are a wonder that You cared so much for me;
That You sent Your only Son, just to set me free;
You have understood me from beginning to the end;
Not only are You Lord to me, but I can call You friend.

November 29

Psalm 139:16 "Your eyes saw my substance, being yet unformed. And in Your book they were all written, The days fashioned for me, When as yet there were none of them."

Lord, how awesome You are that I would be special to You,
That You had planned my days to be many, not few;
Each day You planned were for good things for me;
Written in a book for the angels to see;
So they could watch over me from day to day;
Lighting up my path as I search for my way.

November 30

Psalm 140:13 "Surely the righteous shall give thanks to Your name: The upright shall dwell in Your presence."

I am righteous in Your eyes by the coming of the King,
Giving thanks from my heart, from my mouth hosannas ring;
Today is just another day to lift my Savior's name,
And to the world so lost in sin, His Lordship I'll proclaim;
I will dwell in His presence and be a guiding light;
And to all who will listen, guide them from their plight.

December 1

Luke 1:49,50 "For He who is mighty has done great things for me, and holy is His name. And His mercy is on those who fear Him from generation to generation."

You are mighty Lord and full of grace for me,
You have opened up my eyes for eternity to see;
Your mercy endures for You have paid the cost;
And in each generation You came to save the lost;
My fear of You is turned to love, gently day by day;
Thank You Lord for guiding me through the narrow way.

December 2

Luke 1:68,69 "Blessed is the Lord God of Israel, For He has visited and redeemed His people, And He raised up a horn of salvation for us In the house of His servant David."

Blessed am I, O Lord, in the life I have to live,
For salvation is a gift that only You can give;
You have redeemed me by the power of the Cross;
There is no other God who can bring me back from loss;
For the power has been given from He who sits on high;
And all who will accept You Lord, He will not deny.

December 3

Luke 1:74,75 "To grant us that we, Being delivered from the hand of our enemies, Might serve Him without fear, In holiness and righteousness before Him all the days of our life."

I have been delivered from eternal blight,
Because my Savior came, to be my light;
I will serve Him, spirit, body, and mind;
The ambassador of His hands, gentle and kind;
I will walk in holiness by the power of His grace;
And lift my eyes to heaven to see His gentle face.

December 4

Luke 1:77,78 "To give knowledge of salvation to His people By the remission of their sins, Through the tender mercy of our God, With which the Dayspring from on high has visited us."

Each new morning You are there when I awake,
To walk with me and talk with me in every step I take;
You are freshness in the morning and strength to me at night;
You keep Your presence in my heart to guide to what is right;
And when I fall or stumble along a darkened way;
You are there to lift me up to face another day.

December 5

Luke 1:79 "To give light to those who sit in darkness and the shadow of death, To guide our feet into the way of peace."

You are the way, O Lord, yes, the truth and the light,
Through Your goodness and Your mercy, given me my sight;
You have taken me from darkness and straightened out my path;
Saved me from eternal death and from eternal wrath;
You are guiding my feet along the straight and narrow way;
I will give my life for You, a light for You today.

December 6

Luke 6:20,21 "Then He lifted up His eyes toward His disciples, and said: 'Blessed are you poor, For yours is the kingdom of God. Blessed are you who hunger now, For you shall be filled. Blessed are you who weep now, for you shall laugh.'"

Lord, Your promises are true and forever mine;
Through all my life I am Yours to refine;
For what ever trial may come today;
I know it's for this moment in life's way;
Each day with You shows me blessings untold;
The power of Your love, Your grace to behold.

December 7

Luke 6:31,32 "And just as you want men to do to you, you also do to them likewise."

Lord help me remember to Whom I belong,
A light for You to do no wrong;
Help me lead by example, Your goodness and grace;
Not sitting before others in a higher place;
Help me lead first and with a servant heart give;
To help others grow and a better life live.

December 8

Luke 6:35 "But love your enemies, do good, and lend, hoping for nothing in return; and your reward will be great, and you will be sons of the Most High. For He is kind to the unthankful and evil."

Lord help me grow into the love with which You speak;
A gentler and more giving spirit is what I seek;
And only with Your Spirit could I be kind;
And in those unthankful, goodness find;
For it is not me that wills to help a foe;
But You in me that calls to make it so.

December 9

Luke 6:37 "Judge not, and you shall not be judged. Condemn not, and you shall not be condemned. Forgive, and you will be forgiven."

Lord, help me stand firm in judgement of behavior,
Looking to You, the example of my Savior;
Not looking to the man, but looking to the sin;
That I might help my brother and sister win;
The battle of Your call to walk in Your way;
Leading them to righteousness in You today.

December 10

Luke 6:38 "Give and it will be given to you: good measure, pressed down, shaken together, and running over will be put into your bosom. For with the same measure that you use, it will be measured back to you."

Lord, Your blessings are given without merit,
Following You ensures the Kingdom to inherit;
What should I worry about what I may give;
When You give me all that I need to live;
Even as I give You will return a great measure;
For in my heart I have You as my treasure.

December 11

Luke 6:45 "A good man out of the good treasure of his heart brings forth good; and an evil man out of the evil treasure of his heart brings forth evil. For out of the abundance of the heart his mouth speaks."

Father, make my heart a treasure of abundance for You,
That all that comes forth will be gentle and true;
I am looking for the good in all mankind;
But, without You it is impossible to find;
Help me be a mouth that speaks of good;
Your example in my walk as I know I should.

December 12

Luke 6:47,48 "Whoever comes to Me, and hears My sayings and does them, I will show you whom he is like: He is like a man building a house, who dug deep and laid the foundation on the rock. And when the flood arose, the stream beat vehemently against that house, and could not shake it, for it was founded on the rock."

Jesus You are the Rock of my foundation,
Sent to lift me up in a corrupted creation;
The waters may come causing pain and strife;
But You, O Lord, are the shield in my life;
I will not be overtaken with trial or grief;
For You are my Rock, my shield, and relief."

December 13

Luke 7:22,23 "Jesus answered and said to them, 'Go and tell John the things you have seen and heard: that the blind see, the lame walk, the lepers are cleansed, the deaf hear, the dead are raised, the poor have the gospel preached to them. And blessed is he who is not offended because of Me.'"

O Lord, how wonderful You are in all Your ways,
There are no other gods as the world portrays;
Only You and the power of Your Spirit that came;
And You have not changed, You remain the same;
I am blessed that You healed me from a worldly fall;
And lifted me up to preach the gospel to all.

December 14

Luke 7:50 "Then He said to the woman, 'Your faith has saved you. Go in peace.'"

Father, this is a new day to praise You for Your grace,
Another day to worship You, to stand before Your face;
For each morning You give freshness to the day;
And for whatever may come, You prepare the way;
You have saved me, Lord, because my faith is in You;
It is Your gift of love and not for what I can do.

December 15

Luke 8:16 "No one, when he has lit a lamp, covers it with a vessel or puts it under a bed, but sets it on a lampstand, that those who enter may see the light."

Jesus, You are the light of the world for all to see,
And in You I am a light, for You have set me free;
The world and its darkness claim there is no light;
But believers in You have claimed back their sight;
I will stand on the hill of life and claim You as King;
Till the trumpet sounds and the angels sing.

December 16

Luke 8:47,48 "Now when the woman saw that she was not hidden, she came trembling; and falling down before Him, she declared to Him in the presence of all the people the reason she had touched Him and how she was healed immediately. And He said to her, 'Daughter, be of good cheer; your faith has made you well. Go in peace.'"

Jesus, thank You for taking me out of my hiding place,
And into Your light where I found Your grace;
Where You lifted up my spirit and a will to win;
You gave me new life and redeemed me from sin;
I will keep my eyes on the bright and narrow way;
And I will thank You for healing me day by day.

December 17

Luke 9:23,24 "Then He said to them all, 'If anyone desires to come after Me, let him deny himself, and take up his Cross daily, and follow Me. For whoever desires to save his life will lose it, but whoever loses his life for My sake will save it.'"

Lord it is my desire to follow after You,
There is no other way that I can make it through;
I do not consider worldly life as a life of gain;
But a life without You as a life of pain;
So I will honor the Cross and follow Your way:
As You lead in my journey, day by day.

December 18

Luke 11:9,10 "So I say to you, ask, and it will be given to you; seek, and you will find; knock, and it will be opened to you. For everyone who asks receives, and he who seeks finds, and to him who knocks it will be opened."

Lord Jesus, I have not because I ask not of You,
If I seek and have faith You show Yourself true;
You are blessing and provision of all that is good;
Lord help me to walk in faith as I should;
Each day provides me with new doors to find;
With You as My Savior, so merciful and kind.

December 19

Luke 11:23 "He who is not with Me is against Me, and he who does not gather with Me scatters."

Lord, it is my purpose to gather all for You,
Remind me of just who I am and things that I must do;
Help me gather round me, those who need to know
Help me stand strong and to the weak Your mercy show;
I will follow You and bow my knee in prayer;
Thank You, Lord, for Your grace and always being there.

December 20

Luke 12:2 "For there is nothing covered that will not be revealed, nor hidden that will not be known."

Lord, search my heart for things that should not be,
Things that may not be revealed or things I cannot see;
You know my heart, Lord, and all that should be known;
Mold me and make me and claim me for Your own;
There is nothing in my life that You do not know;
Thank You Lord for loving me and helping me to grow.

December 21

Luke 12:29,30 "And do not seek what you should eat or what you should drink, nor have an anxious mind. For all these things the nations of the world seek after, and your Father knows that you need these things."

From morning to morning, You meet every need,
Remind me of Your provision and keep me from greed;
There is no reason for a worldly anxious mind;
For everything needed, in You I find;
The world is discontent, for You it cannot see;
But I have no wonder, in You is where I'll be.

December 22

Luke 16:13 "No servant can serve two masters; for either he will hate the one and love the other, or else he will be loyal to the one and despise the other. You can not serve God and mammon."

Jesus, You are Lord, all others I despise,
I will walk in Your way, I will not compromise;
Today is the day I lift my voice in praise;
To live an example of Your righteous ways;
I will look to heaven and lift my head up high;
Speak the name of Jesus, the Name I'll not deny.

December 23

Luke 17:3 "Take heed to yourselves. If your brother sins against you, rebuke him; and if he repents, forgive him."

Father, help me be firm in my faith, but gentle in deed,
Reminding myself and others of Your word to heed;
If I must rebuke a brother out of line;
Let it be with mercy and of You a sign;
Repentance is key to a life filled with grace;
Forgiveness is key to my eternal place.

December 24

Luke 17:20,21 "Now when He was asked by the Pharisees when the kingdom of God would come, He answered them and said, 'The kingdom of God does not come with observation; nor will they say, 'See here!' or 'See There!' For indeed, the kingdom of God is within you."

You have told me in Scripture that I am Your home,
That I am a living vessel no longer to roam;
But established in You, Where the Holy Spirit dwells;
A work without walls and no Sunday bells;
A kingdom of one, yet a kingdom for all;
Each one in Your Spirit, heeding Your call.

December 25

Luke 2:11 "For there is born to you this day in the city of David a Savior, who is Christ the Lord."

The day I was born, You had a plan for me,
That through the birth of Christ, You would set me free;
That I would be a vessel to carry on Your plan;
And through the Holy Spirit, speak Christ to every man;
Fill me Lord with power, by Your Spirit from within;
To lead by Your example, Your light among all men.

December 26

Luke 19:9,10 "And Jesus said to him, 'Today salvation has come to this house, because he also is a son of Abraham; for the Son of Man has come to seek and to save that which was lost.'"

Father, You sent Your Son to save those lost,
To be the final sacrifice to bare mans cost;
There is no greater love for all to see;
Than the cost of the Son to set us free;
You have saved the lost from eternal doom;
To dwell forever in Your upper room.

December 27

Luke 21:33,34 "Heaven and earth will pass away, but My words will by no means pass away. But take heed to yourselves, lest your hearts be weighed down with carousing, drunkenness, and cares of this life, and that Day come on you unexpectedly."

Father, day by day I will keep my eyes on You,
I will take heed to my words and what I do;
I will not let worldly ways tempt me to loss;
I'm reminded of what Jesus did on the Cross;
He secured me a place and I am heaven bound;
No greater love is there to be found.

December 28

Luke 22:61 "And the Lord turned and looked at Peter. Then Peter remembered the word of the Lord, how He said to him, 'Before the rooster crows, you will deny Me three times.'"

Father, help my life speak in righteousness alone,
That my life would not deny the grace You have shown;
Each morning I wake I will lift up Your name;
Giving You praises for the reason You came.
May the love in my heart be an overflow;
Of Your love in me to all I'll show.

December 29

Luke 24:45 "And He opened of understanding, that they might comprehend the Scriptures."

Lord, You have risen and I am no longer blind,
You have softened my heart and opened my mind;
To the things of God that lead the way I live;
To learn to love and that its blessed to give;
Lead me on Lord till the day I see Your face;
To a life of victory until Your final grace.

December 30

1 Thess. 5:23,24 "Now may the God of peace Himself sanctify you completely; and may your whole spirit, soul, and body be preserved blameless at the coming of our Lord Jesus Christ. He who calls you is faithful, who also will do it."

Father, You are the reason I will be held blameless,
For the Son has come and made me shameless;
I am redeemed and made complete in the Son;
Through all life's trials, I have already won;
He who has called me is faithful to abide;
Forever with me and walking by my side.

December 31

I Tim. 1:17 "Now to the King eternal, immortal, invisible, to God who alone is wise, be honor and glory forever and ever. Amen.

This is the final call of my love for You,
To my Savior, my Lord, the One always true;
I pledge allegiance to the Sacrificial Lamb;
To the one I call Master, to the great I Am;
Today and forever I will pledge to You, my all;
And praise You and honor You for giving me Your call.
Amen.

About the Author

Rev. Hausmann and his family have served in the ministry since 1985, primarily as missionaries, living and ministering in Indonesia, from 1985-1999, the largest predominantly Muslim country in the world. In addition to church planting and pastoring, he served as an administrator for a Christian school system in Indonesia and as Chaplain for a Christian hospital there. He is a published poet and song writer, and has traveled extensively in Asia as a gospel singer with YASKI/FEBC (Far East Broadcasting Corp.) and as a conference speaker. His ministry emphasis is the life changing power of Jesus Christ as Lord through the indwelling presence of the Holy Spirit. He encourages standing firm in the faith at all times and uses various examples of personal experience. God's ministry through him also focuses on building strong families and proper raising of children in the light of God's Word.

He was a successful Domestic and International Human Resources Administrator before his acceptance of Christ and subsequent ministry. His own testimony is a powerful message of God's love, grace, and provision.

Rev. Hausmann is a licensed and ordained minister and is presently ministering at April Sound Church, Montgomery, Texas. He is also President/Founder of Whitewing Ministries Intl., an international ministry promoting the Gospel of Jesus Christ through music and word.